DEVOTIONS
for MARRIED
COUPLES

*One Year of Weekly Devotions to Deepen
Your Spiritual Connection with God and Each Other*

MANDY & JOEL SHROCK

CONTENTS

OCTOBER

NOVEMBER

DECEMBER

APPENDIX

FOREWORD

If you are familiar with the devotional book, *Life in Abundance,* you will notice half of its devotions are very similar to the devotions in this book, with the exception of added marriage application. While they are similar, it is worthwhile to read both books — *Life In Abundance* on your own, and *Marriage In Abundance Devotions for Married Couples* with your spouse. This way, you will glean the most — personal growth with God and spiritual growth as a couple!

INTRODUCTION

This book of couples' devotions is just "one part of a whole" for Marriage In Abundance's approach to a better marriage. Our goal at Marriage In Abundance is to help couples discover just how deep and meaningful their marriage relationship can be. For best results, this book is to be used in conjunction with *Marriage In Abundance's Date Plans for Married Couples, Marriage Challenges for Him* and *Marriage Challenges for Her*. To find access to the full program, visit www.marriageinabundance.com.

Here's an overview of what you'll find through Marriage In Abundance:

- **Date Plans for Married Couples** — weekly date plans for fostering creative, engaging, quality time together.

- **Couples' Devotions** — weekly studies to deepen your spiritual connection with God and each other.

- **Marriage Challenges** — weekly suggestions for showing love to one another more effectively, plus monthly suggestions for eliminating unhealthy styles of conflict resolution. As our schedules become overloaded, marital connection takes a backseat. The marriage challenges bring intentionality to meeting one another's needs and desires and spicing up the romance.

If following Marriage In Abundance's approach to a better marriage, each aspect is to be completed once a week — the date, the devotion, and the marriage challenge. The marriage challenges are to be completed separate from the dates and devotions as they are meant to slip romance into our busy, everyday routines. However, there is more flexibility with the dates and devotions. Some people choose to do the couple's devotions while on their date together—connecting once during the week. Others like to break it up and do their devotions one night of the week and go on their date another night of the week—connecting twice during the week. Choose what works best for you.

We—Joel and Mandy—are excited to dive into God's blueprints with you and help you discover a deeper level of intimacy like you've never experienced before!

JANUARY

MARRIAGE —
WHAT'S THE POINT?

*"For this reason a man will leave his father and
mother and be united to his wife, and the two will
become one flesh." This is a profound mystery — but
I am talking about Christ and the church.*

EPHESIANS 5:31-32

What is the purpose of marriage? It has many benefits: companionship, enjoyment, protection, provision for needs, and procreation. While those are all great perks, any of those reasons alone are not enough to sustain a marriage. If we marry for the purpose of finding happiness or with expectations for our spouse to meet our needs, we will not have the "happily ever after" we anticipated. If these are our reasons for marrying, when our spouse does not fulfill our needs and expectations (and let's be honest, no one can), we will seek satisfaction through other relationships or outlets. The marriage that depends solely on each other will hang on by a thread, if at all.

Furthermore, relying on a person for fulfillment is a form of idolatry — sin number one of the Ten Commandments. Idolatry is when we love, treasure, and desire for something or someone more than we love, treasure and desire for God. So, when we find our hearts unsatisfied by people, we must realize we were longing for the wrong thing, from the wrong one. It was God who we should've sought. Only God can satisfy. An adjustment to our perspective regarding the purpose for marriage is necessary.

Let's go back to the beginning. God created man, then said it wasn't good for man to be alone. So, God made woman using a piece of the man. A part of him was literally removed to form her (Genesis 2:18-23). Man was separated—a partial withdrawal—leaving him incomplete. Moreover, God created both male and female in his own image—not just man, not just woman—both, the image of God (Genesis 1:27). Some theorize, when man and woman come together in marriage, they are reconnecting what was once separated, causing what was simply a part, to become whole again. In addition, when we are joined together in marriage, our union more clearly reflects the image of God.

Scripture compares marriage to the union between Christ and the Church. Jesus—the bridegroom—and the Church—his bride. Furthermore, we are told when our long-anticipated Christ returns for us, we will be united with him in a "wedding ceremony" (Ephesians 5:31-32, Revelation 19:7-9, 21:1-2). Just as Jesus came to serve and to give up his life for his bride, so are we to serve one another and to give up our lives for one another. A God-reflecting marriage looks more like service and sacrifice than seeking fulfillment. Nurturing our marriage through serving our spouse is parallel to our relationship with Christ and when sacrifice is our stance, our marriage will more accurately reflect the image of God.

Self-sacrifice is not a foreign concept in Christianity. All Christ-followers, married or not, are required to deny themselves for a greater cause (Luke 9:23). Marriage follows the same principle. Once we lose ourselves, we find real life (Matthew 10:39). In the same way, once we die to our selfish desires, only then will our marriage thrive. Selfishness and marriage cannot coexist.

To recap: our marriage purpose is to, as a unified team, reflect the image of God, resemble the union of Jesus and the church, to prepare one another for the upcoming "wedding ceremony," to sharpen one another, to snuff out our selfishness, to spur one another toward purity and righteousness, to cheer one another on, so that we can continue this spiritual battle and fight the enemy together with one power-packed punch!

Discuss It: What do service and sacrifice look like in your marriage? What past sacrifices have you made that strengthened your marriage? What do you still need to sacrifice to further strengthen your marriage? What selfish desire needs to die to give your marriage new life?

Pray Over It: Father, thank you for caring enough about us to provide us with each other. Show us areas of sacrifice we each need to make for our marriage to grow stronger. Please change our perspective of marriage from *what can this give me* to *how can this make each of us grow.* Amen.

OUR DESIRE FOR MORE

The thief comes only to steal and kill and destroy. I came that they may have life and have it abundantly.

JOHN 10:10 ESV

Life. It has left us feeling much to be desired. Because there is. We're missing something. Because we've been broken into and robbed. There is a thief who has come to "steal, kill, and destroy" all that God intends for us: life abundant with love, joy, and peace. This thief's crusade to rob us began in the Garden of Eden when he lied to us and we believed him, exchanging Plan A for Plan B. Plan A crumbled into ruins when humankind bit into the wrong advice, thinking there was a better way.

A little refresher course: We were created as perfect people and placed in a perfect setting, the Garden of Eden. The first two chapters of Genesis tell us of the life that was meant to be—no pain, no sorrow, no death, perfect connection with God, and perfect union with one another. But rather quickly (chapter 3), things went very wrong. Despite warning, we chose the wrong path—and God set Plan B into motion. Now we breathe, and attempt to have life, in an imperfect world of our own making, a world destroyed by greed. In the inner recesses of our hearts, we long for what we once had. It is a longing placed in each of us by God, himself. A longing he would have fulfilled perfectly in Plan A.

When sin entered the world, along came discontentment with life and hiding from God, the only One who could fill the hunger of our hearts. The longing within us cries out for more, for what was lost in the Garden, for that perfect world. Our expectations for "more" carry on. By design, we are always searching, sometimes subconsciously, for that perfect world that no longer exists.

Typically, we see dissatisfaction as a negative thing, a part of our sinful nature, but what we don't realize is that our *desire for more* is God's design for Plan B. God expects us to seek more out of life. The problem is, we displace our *desire for more* with things that don't ever satisfy, the things of this broken world. We want a bigger house, a fancier car, a higher-paying job, more vacation time, a spouse who is more romantic and bickers less, the perfect kids (you know, the ones we see so perfectly displayed on social media), and more money than we need. We compare ourselves to others who we think have "everything" until we find out Mr. & Mrs. Perfect HaveItAll are equally discontent. There is still something lacking, something lost.

Many times, in our attempts to fulfill our *desire for more*, we expect our spouse to play a role that can only be filled by God. Jerry Maguire's statement, "You complete me," has become our aspiration (*Jerry Maguire,* 1996).[1] Though spouses come with benefits—companionship, sexual intimacy, financial security, humor for the hard days, a shoulder to cry on, and practical advice—our husband's or wife's capacity to completely fulfill *all* our needs is sorely lacking.

Were Jesus's needs met by any one person? It sounds ridiculous to think of Jesus depending on people to fill his emotional tank, crying himself to sleep because unkind things were said to him, leaving him feeling pretty down on himself. Jesus spent long amounts of time in the Father's presence, being filled with the Spirit. That's how he endured walking this earth. And that's how he tells us we are to endure this earth (Matthew 6:33, John 15:1-5, Luke 10:38-42). Jesus was let down by people multiple times. He knows people will let you and me down too, but *God* never will. He doesn't want us to depend on others to meet our needs. He wants our dependence on him alone.

Although only God completely fulfills our souls, we're not off the hook in serving one another. It brings God joy when we reach beyond ourselves and meet another's need. God commands us over and over to take care of each other's needs. The Bible is full of "one another" verses instructing us to meet each other's needs — fifty-nine of them to be precise. To name a few: love one another, be devoted to one another, instruct one another, serve one another, forgive one another, carry one another's burdens, be kind and compassionate to one another, spur one another on toward love and good deeds, encourage one another, and pray for one another (John 13:34, Romans 12:10, Romans 15:14, Galatians 5:13, Ephesians 4:32, Galatians 6:2, Hebrews 10:24, 25, James 5:16).

Another command we are given is to make disciples (Matthew 28:19-20). Most of the time, we look at discipleship as something that happens outside the home, but discipleship happens inside the home as well. Marriage is a form of discipleship as it teaches us the tough disciplines of service, forgiveness, humility, and perseverance to build something that takes a lifetime. It's a form of discipleship completely different than any other type of discipleship. The world looks at marriage and asks, *How is my marriage serving me?,* but we should be looking at it and asking, *How am I using my marriage to serve God?*

God may use our spouse to provide for some of our needs or to bring about the change he wants in us. And, in turn, we may use our marriage to serve and surrender to God by providing for our spouse's needs. But marriage will not provide all our needs. It will not complete us.

Whether our spouse tries hard to fill all our needs or stopped trying a long time ago, God longs for our relationship with him to be our primary source of satisfaction. God knows we are human, we fail to fit the bill, and it's impossible for us to *completely* meet another's needs. The emptiness we feel when we are failed by another person is there for a reason: to point us to God. We're meant to desire more life. And God is happy to oblige. He longs to satisfy.

What if we went into marriage, not looking for what we can "get" out of it, but how it can change us for the better? What if we sought not to be completed by a human, but to be sharpened by a human and completed by God?

Discuss It: What unfulfilled desires plague you? In what ways do you attempt to satisfy that desire? In what ways have you unreasonably expected your spouse to fulfill you in ways only God can? Consider releasing this expectation and praying God would satisfy this need.

Pray Over It: Father, we know this life we're living is not Plan A. We're feeling it. We've been discontent and searching for more but, usually, we look to the things that will never satisfy. Even though we may provide for some of each other's desires, we realize we have only a limited capacity to completely satisfy one another's souls. Remind us not to expect more from each other than we can give. Teach us to look only to you for complete satisfaction. Help us to understand true abundant life through experience. Fill us with all the right things until we have attained true, abundant life. Amen.

THE THIEF STEALS, KILLS, AND DESTROYS

The thief comes only to steal and kill and destroy. I came that they may have life and have it abundantly.

JOHN 10:10 ESV

Our enemy, Satan the Swindler, wants what is not his, including our souls. If he can't have that, he'll try to rob us of the abundant life we were meant to have.

The Greek word for *steal* is *klepto,* which is an artful way of pickpocketing undetectably. What we had is gone before we realize what happened. It's a cunning technique of thievery, unnoticed by those being robbed blind.

If Satan can't sneaky-steal it, his next maneuver is to kill. The Greek word for *kill* used in this verse is *thuo,* which is to sacrifice, to give up something that is precious. If he can't steal it, he will cunningly convince us to give it up. Adam and Eve were duped by this kind of persuasion and sometimes so are we. What looks like a slice of heaven, promising to improve our lives is actually destructive. These can be things like having an affair, cheating our way to the top, or taking revenge on another. Those tricky things that look so enticing come back to bite us in the butt with the venom of a serpent. If he can't steal God's blessings from us, he will try to convince us to forfeit them.

The third strategy of Satan is to destroy, which is from the Greek word *apollumi,* meaning to ruin or waste. If Satan can't steal it or convince us to hand it over, he will ruin it. This thief wants to destroy our lives, most importantly our souls and eternities with God. However, if we are in Christ, the thief cannot have our souls.

Satan is a sore loser. Dissatisfied with the off-limit status of our souls, he then robs us of the enjoyment of life here on earth. He steals our joy, our peace, and our trust in the Lord. Satan blinds us to the purpose of our existence and diverts our focus, so we take our eyes off Jesus. Then Satan dishes out to us trials, distractions, obstacles, and interruptions until, in utter discouragement and defeat, we forget who we are in Christ.

One of Satan's favorite things to steal, kill, and destroy is marriage. Satan hates marriage, as it is symbolic of our relationship with God. If Satan can distort our view of the marriage relationship, what may follow is a skewed perspective of ourselves — the bride — in relationship with Christ — the Bridegroom (Isaiah 54:5, Ephesians 5:25-27, Revelation 19:7, Revelation 21:2).

Satan also destroys marriages because marriage is an accelerator to the sanctification process. There is nothing like marriage to confront our selfishness and grow us into Christ-like servants. It stretches us to practice patience over a quick-temper, forgiveness over grudges, and sacrifice over selfish pleasures. God can both bless and grow us through marriage. With all the power a marriage possesses, of course Satan wants to destroy it!

When playing a game of football, it's important to keep your eyes on the end zone. You know you may be blind-sided, but by keeping your eyes on the end zone, you charge forward with determined focus. Marriage is even more important than a game, it's a vow you made to God. Satan will blind-side your marriage. Expect that. When it happens, keep your eyes on Christ and the vow you made to God and then run hard to get your touchdown.

Hold on tight to your faith, the truths of the Word, and your marriage. Lying is Satan's only power over you. Don't bite! Don't allow him to convince you to give up what he has no power to take away.

Discuss It: Aside from marriage, what has the master thief ruined, stolen from you, or talked you into forfeiting with a convincing lie that your life would be better? How can you hold tight to your faith and to truth? How can you catch the enemy in his lies before you bite into them? In what ways is Satan attempting to steal, kill, and destroy your marriage? How has your marriage blessed you? How has it sharpened you? What does it look like to hold tightly to your marriage?

Pray Over It: Bridegroom, we look forward to the day we are united with you. We've had so much taken from us—so much stolen, sacrificed, and ruined. We've been told we are not valuable to you. We recognize it for the lie that it is. The enemy wants us to give up our faith and the abundant life you gave us. He wants to take what you created us to desire. He wants to ruin our marriage. Help us to recognize it for the lie that it is. Help us to hold tight and not allow what is ours to be stolen, killed, or destroyed. Amen.

LIFE ABUNDANTLY

*The thief comes only to steal and kill and destroy. I came
that they may have life and have it abundantly.*

JOHN 10:10 ESV

Let's say you are given a vacation package. You have multiple choices and they all cost you nothing. Are you going to choose the small neighboring town, stay in the motel the police are well-acquainted with, and eat at the truck stop? Or are you going to choose the package offering a private island in the Caribbean with accommodations including a luxury spa and your own private chef?

Spiritually speaking, Jesus has an offer. It is only an offer — not automatically given. His offer is, "that they may have life, and have it more abundantly." "They may have" is referring to potential, to what is possible, to what is available for the taking. It's a choice we don't have to take, and some of us don't. Some of us are saved, but walking around as though dead inside, as if we've chosen the small-town motel package, not having taken advantage of the abundant life offered to us here and now.

Which package have you chosen? Do you want to live a lame life — fruitless and unsatisfying? Or do you want to take hold of the abundant, satisfying life offered to you?

Before we begin to chase after lavish homes, luxury cars, world-wide travel, and more money than we know what to do with, we need to recognize what Jesus meant by "abundant life." We learn in 1 Corinthians 1:26-29 that God's main priority for us is not monetary wealth and high position. Paradoxically, sometimes following Christ grants us more troubles. In more places in the world than we want to think about, following Christ can get us arrested or even killed! It's obviously not a lack of problems Jesus is offering us. The abundant life is a state of being from within, not the result of external circumstances. Jesus's desire is to increase our "wealth" not monetarily but in deep soul-satisfying ways.

Take King Solomon. He had all the material things one could ever imagine, yet, found it all meaningless (Ecclesiastes 5:10-15). On the contrary, many others in the Bible lived lives of struggle, suffering and pain, yet were able to sing in prison, march confidently into battle with the odds stacked against them, and walk into a fiery furnace with hope. We think *we* were dealt an unfair hand in life. Many believers throughout history were tortured, imprisoned, stoned, sawed in two, destitute, treated unfairly, beaten, and left homeless. Yet it was these same struggling people who spoke of a peace beyond understanding and a deep-seated joy. That is what's there for the taking. That is abundant life.

The "abundant life" Jesus offers includes: joy and peace despite circumstances; patience and wisdom to make the right choices; strength and encouragement to keep going when we're weary; the ability to see truth; freedom from the bondage of sin; rest for our souls; freedom from guilt through forgiveness; healing for our broken spirits; the ability to see good come from bad; guidance when confused; the ability to see God's hand move and work; and love and grace to extend to others who try our patience and break our hearts.

Bringing Jesus into our marriage brings it to abundance as well. Just as following Christ can grant us more trials, our marriage may be attacked even harder when we're following Christ. But remember, the abundance God gives is a state of being within. When we go through hard times, we have joy, peace, patience, wisdom, perseverance, truth, forgiveness, and healing. If we hang on to God's truths and accept the abundant life he offers, the adversities won't destroy our marriage. They will make it stronger.

Recall the differing vacation packages offered. Marriages come in a variety of packages as well. One package offered is the marriage that functions as roommates—tag-teaming to raise the kids and to pay the bills but ignoring the need for emotional connection and physical intimacy. The other package is the intimate union in which both spouses are fully connected and striving to support one another.

Which end of the spectrum does your marriage tend to fall? Marriage takes work, but the compensation is worth the effort. A strong, intimate, healthy marriage is the vacation package that pays for itself.

If you want to choose the "intimate" package over the "roommate" package, here are small ways to put in the effort: be intentional about making the marriage a priority, date one another, create the time to connect in meaningful conversation regularly, communicate both the big things and the small things, offer compassion even when you don't completely understand, provide affectionate touches daily, provide for one another's sexual needs, look past minor annoyances, offer frequent encouragement, let go of "being right," and choose your spouse over yourself.

The abundant life—it's there for the taking. We simply need to accept.

Discuss It: Look again through the examples of the kind of abundant life Jesus offers. What aspects of abundant life may be lacking from your life? What steps will you take to accept this gift? Look over the ideas for choosing the "intimate" marriage package in the last paragraph. Choose at least one to focus your energy.

Pray Over It: Jesus, thank you for your gracious offer of abundant life, a life of triumph and fulfillment. Help us stop chasing things that have the false appearance of a better life but leave us feeling empty. May we be radically changed and profoundly satisfied. Help us to focus on [list out the area(s) you are choosing to be intentional about improving]. God, please deepen the intimacy in our marriage. Amen.

FEBRUARY

KNOWN &
FULLY LOVED

*For you created my inmost being; you knit me together in my mother's
womb. I praise you because I am fearfully and wonderfully made;
your works are wonderful. I know that full well. My frame was not
hidden from you when I was made in the secret place, when I was
woven together in the depths of the earth. Your eyes saw my unformed
body; all the days ordained for me were written in your book before
one of them came to be. How precious to me are your thoughts, God!
How vast is the sum of them! Were I to count them, they would
outnumber the grains of sand—when I awake, I am still with you.*

Psalm 139:13-18

Do you ever think about God and wonder, *Does God ever think
about me as well?* These verses promise that he does, indeed! He
formed you in the darkness of the womb, he sees your days before
they even come about, and his thoughts concerning you outnumber
the grains of sand. Stop and think about that. Have you been to the
beach? Could you count the grains of sand in a bucket? How about
the sand covering the entire earth? Impossible! Yet this is the number outweighed by the thoughts of God *about you*! Therefore, God
thinks about you more than you think about him!

God created you, knit you together in your mother's womb, not
just your physical body, but your personality, characteristics, emotions, and mental makeup. You are exactly what you were created to
be. Every aspect of you was created with intention.

Verse 14 says, "I am fearfully and wonderfully made…" "Fear" is a
negative emotion. It is the idea or sense that something bad or harmful

is about to happen. So, what does it mean that you were fearfully and wonderfully made? The Hebrew word for *fearfully* used here is derived from the root *yara,* which expresses a reverent awe. It is mind blowing that the God who created you is in awe of you—even *admires* you.

No one knows you better than your Creator. He knows your every thought, every habit, every action you've ever done, and will do! Even then, after knowing your depths, God is still in awe of you. If God is astonished by you, should you not accept yourself as the treasure God knows you are? Should you not conduct yourself as one revered by the Creator? Maybe, instead, you feel worthless, live as if you are trash, and have allowed your warped sense of worth to direct the way you treat yourself and those around you. Maybe your skewed self-image is leading to your own demise.

It is a journey to fully embrace God's love and acceptance—to move the knowledge that you are a cherished treasure from your head into your heart, and then into your actions—to live like you're loved and accepted.

Yes, you astonish the Creator. And so does your spouse. Look at your spouse in light of that truth. Every time you look down on her, you are mentally belittling someone who impresses God. Every time you insult him, you are insulting someone who blows God's mind. Every time you hold a grudge against him, you are holding a grudge against someone God cherishes. When you deny the worth of her, it offends God.

What if we always viewed our spouse as a precious child of God, a beloved brother or sister in Christ? We would listen a whole lot more. Rather than shutting down their thoughts and opinions in a desperate attempt to get them to see our own, we would show respect and take their views into consideration. There would be less screaming, fewer insults, less condescension, and less neglect. There would be more respect and acceptance. We would understand full well we have not walked a mile in their shoes—shoes of their past and learned thought processes. Our judgement and disrespect would be stopped in their tracks.

It's tough to get to the place where we can love and accept ourselves—an even tougher mission to love and accept the person who, at times, brings out the worst in us. Our responsibility is to love and show respect to everyone, including our spouse. We don't get to decide if they are worthy of our love. God already decided they are.

Discuss It: Is it hard for you to believe God thinks about you? How would your life be different if you came to truly believe that he treasures you and his thoughts of you are unceasing and innumerable? Imagine which aspects and qualities of your spouse God admires, then tell your spouse what they would be. No need to discuss this next question, but simply take a moment to reflect on it: If you fully understood God's love for your spouse, how would it change the way you treat him or her? It is hard for us to move the knowledge of God's love from our heads to our hearts: How can you help your spouse do this?

Pray Over It: God, thank you that your thoughts are on us. Although sometimes it feels we were simply created and then forgotten, we've learned your thoughts persist on us. Help us to grasp the depth of that love, to see each other the way you see us, and to love each other the way you love us. Please give us a new perspective on our worth—*your* perspective on our worth. May it change us, the way we live, and the way we treat one another. Amen.

BEAUTY IN OUR
CRUSHED CLAY POTS

*But we have this treasure in jars of clay to show that
this all-surpassing power is from God and not from
us. We are hard pressed on every side, but not crushed;
perplexed, but not in despair; persecuted, but not
abandoned; struck down, but not destroyed.*

2 CORINTHIANS 4:7-9

In the ancient near east, clay jars were used to store one's wealth. When saving for something costly, like a field, people would bury the clay pots with their coins inside. These clay pots were commonplace and had little value, but they were made to hold a treasure. This is the comparison Paul uses to describe *us*. Unlike a gold treasure chest adorned with jewels, clay pots are plain and simple. Similarly, we are nothing outstanding. It's the treasure inside giving us worth, and that treasure is God himself.

Hard pressed. That is the way God expects us to live. He never promised our lives would be easy. In fact, we're guaranteed trials (John 16:33). We don't even get to choose the trials. We just ride the waves coming at us. The hope this Scripture brings is that even though we are pressed from every side, we can have confidence we won't be destroyed in the process. Many pots break under pressure, but not us! In fact, God uses our hardships to show others we are different and to show himself through us. God wants to show himself to the world through a different attitude and a different way of reacting to suffering. Others who see us hard-pressed, going through trials yet not breaking, can see we have a superhuman strength in an atmosphere of great pressure. We are still holding on to our joy and peace. We show others good can come out of suffering.

Jesus abandoned his place in Heaven and came to earth as a "clay jar." He was crushed for our transgressions, hard-pressed on the cross, felt the physical pain from beatings and the emotional pain of rejection. He was willing to lose his life and trusted God not only to bring it back but to bring about something significant from his suffering. God came through! Jesus's death and resurrection were so significant that we are still astounded by him 2,000 years later! The power was not in his "clay jar," the earthly body that contained him, but in his message.

Just as Jesus died so we could be given life, when we die to our selfish desires, others are given life. We are called to superhuman acts like loving our enemies, forsaking vengeance, and doing good to those who don't deserve it.

Though marriage is meant for improving our lives, sometimes marriage crushes us. We must die to our selfish desires, love and serve our spouse when he or she hasn't been acting in a way deserving of our love, and forgive our spouse even while we hurt. Our "pressing" is where God speaks with the loudest, most impactful message.

Let's remember this: Though we are hard-pressed, we are not abandoned. God doesn't leave us there in our pain. He brings joy in the morning. He makes beauty from ashes. He turns our mourning to a joyous blessing. He takes a heart of despair and transforms it to praise. These are promised to us in Isaiah 61:3. Just as death brings new life, the sacrifices we make for our marriage breathe into it new life.

Discuss It: Can you think of someone who is an ace at demonstrating joy and peace throughout their suffering? What do you think gives them this strength? What ways, in past times of distress, have you seen positive come from pain? What specific troubles are you going through right now? How do you think God can use this to show himself powerful? In what way might Satan be trying to crush your marriage? What needs to die for your marriage to take on new life?

Pray Over It: Father, God, even though it feels we might be crushed, thank you for always pulling us through. Thank you that our suffering is not wasted. Thank you for giving us such a significant purpose of holding this treasure inside us. Help us to trust you are going to make something good from our difficulties and pain. Continue to carry us through the ups and downs in our marriage. May our marriage be a megaphone for you to blare your beautiful message. Amen.

LOVE NEVER FAILS

*Love never fails. But where there are prophecies, they
will cease; where there are tongues, they will be stilled;
where there is knowledge, it will pass away.*

1 Corinthians 13:8

What makes a man or woman "godly"? What would you say is the standard of measurement for a truly spiritual person? The amount of money he gives? How often she goes to church? How many poor people she fed? How elaborate are his prayers? How many Scriptures she posted on social media? The Corinthian Church believed the measurement of spirituality was the demonstration of spiritual gifts. In fact, they were so busy assessing their lives by their spiritual gifts, they forgot about love. It's not an uncommon thought. We've been to some churches in this century who use spiritual gifts to determine if one is truly a believer. If that's not it, what is the gauge that registers some degree of godliness? Paul teaches us in 1 Corinthians 13 that gauge is love. Jesus taught us the same thing, "By this everyone will know that you are my disciples, if you love one another" (John 13:35). Love, pure and simple.

Loving well is the gold standard, not whether we sing well or teach well. Why is this? Why does God determine our spirituality by the way we love and not by the good deeds we accomplish or the way we use our gifts? Paul answers this question clearly. It is because spiritual gifts are temporary; they will pass away. But love is enduring. Spiritual gifts are only a small part of the whole, while love is complete. Paul contrasts this God-rooted act — love — with the things that will not last, the things that do have an expiration date. The temporary spiritual gifts are designed to lead us to love, which never ends.

The gifts of knowledge, prophecy, and tongues are important God-given gifts with the purpose of growing the church. But they have a time and place, and that time and place has an end. They were never intended for eternity.

Love never fails — never ends. It doesn't accumulate in our hearts until we give it away, depleting our reservoir of love. It's doesn't operate as a filling and emptying. Many times, we don't even have it to give when we need to give it. When we're running on empty, if we simply ask God for this power we lack, he will always supply us with the power to love as he loves, but sometimes not until the very moment we need it.

Oftentimes, we feel we have nothing to give, certainly not the selfless, unconditional love God has called us to give. But he did not call us to a love we can't extend. If our hearts are willing and if we ask, God will empower us to love well. To say we can't extend love to the unlovable is to say God's love isn't enough.

There are times we reach the end of our rope and we don't have one more ounce of love to offer. Then, God steps in to provide us a little bit more love to give — supernatural self-control, kindness, and patience — all certainly outside our own capacity. There are times we conjure up in our head all the things we want to say to someone and we're ready to go "tell them off." But before we open our mouth, the Holy Spirit intervenes and softens our words with compassion and gentleness. There are times our children push our buttons until we reach our boiling point but instead of lashing out at them, we suddenly get a grip on our control and speak calmly. Sometimes we don't have it in us to serve the ungrateful, high-maintenance person one more time, but then we're reminded and given strength to go one more mile (Matthew 5:40-41). There are times we decide there's no way we can let go of a personal injustice one more time, but we are surprised by the strength within us to forgive, yet again, one more time. It's at these times we think we used our last drop of love, but we're astonished to find there is love beyond ourselves, a "rainy-day fund" of God-empowered love, renewing our heart. The powerful stream of God's pure love carried us along. Love never fails.

Sometimes, the one we feel we just can't love any longer is our spouse. The ones we love dearest have the greatest capacity to hurt us. Sometimes, we are wronged, pushed to anger beyond words, or hurt beyond our ability to cope. Sometimes, patience and kindness are so far-fetched, they are unattainable in our own strength. But God is able. He has enough love for our spouse and is willing to let it flow through us when we allow it.

As we get in the habit of realizing how powerless we are to love on our own, asking for a supply of God's love to give, dying to self, and living for loving others, we begin to find ease in this cycle. The more we practice giving love away, the more effortless it becomes. Receiving from God and giving to others is a cycle that becomes more natural and habitual the longer we practice. If our spirituality is "measured" as the Corinthian church believed, and if Christians are known by our love as Paul taught, may it be found true that our love covers our spouse well.

Love never fails. There is a bottomless supply. We need only tap in.

Discuss It: Have you ever put knowledge above love? What about teaching or exercising spiritual gifts? How do we lose focus of love when we're "doing things" for the Kingdom? Is there something that needs to change in your life to prioritize love to the very top where God has made it? Think of a time you realized you had no love to give on your own and then God clearly empowered you to love. No need for discussion, simply reflection for this: When is your spouse most difficult to love? Take a mental note—these are the moments you need to tap into God's unending reservoir of love.

Pray Over It: Loving Father, thank you for your unlimited supply of love. Our ability to love is so insufficient. Please provide us with the capacity to love beyond our own feelings and limited scope. Continue to pour your fuel of love into us so we can demonstrate your supernatural love to all, even those who are difficult to love, and especially to each other. May everyone know we are yours because we have loved well. May that love point them to you. Amen

FORGIVE

*Make allowance for each other's faults, and forgive
anyone who offends you. Remember, the Lord
forgave you, so you must forgive others.*

Colossians 3:13 nlt

Broken people have sharp edges. We have all been broken to some extent, therefore, we all have shards like little glass daggers pointing outward, ready to jab others. Even if we go about our day trying to keep our shards from touching others, unintentionally we bump another, hurting them. We so much need the forgiveness of God and others. Fortunately, we have been forgiven by God. Jesus then requires us to extend that forgiveness to others as well. Forgiveness is not simply a suggestion. It is a firm commandment.

"Being resentful, they say, is like taking poison and waiting for the other person to die."[2] Chew on that for a minute. Who suffers when we don't forgive? Possibly the one who wronged us. However, to a deeper extent, *we* decay under the poison of our own unforgiveness. Anger, resentment, and hate become our prisons. And who has control over our prisons? The one who imprisoned us. You and me. We make the decision to either stay in our self-created prison, or to be free, not giving others the control of our emotions.

In any healthy relationship, forgiveness is essential. We can't simply chuck every relationship that causes us hurt. We'd be chucking them out right and left. We must operate with forgiveness. No tight family became genuinely close without hard-fought forgiveness. No long-term best friends became chummy without the offering and acceptance of an occasional olive branch. And no marriage celebrates a fifty-year-anniversary without the mercy of forgiveness. If we want any valuable relationship, forgiveness is essential.

Does forgiveness mean we continue in an abusive relationship, without protective boundaries in place? Absolutely, not. It means we're not going to hold a grudge. We're not going to bring it up again. We're not going to desire hardships for the one who hurt us. Forgiveness means we are going to wish our offender well. This is hard to do! I have found that praying *for* people helps me let go of my grudges. Praying good things over their life — success in their career, joy in their heart, fulfilling relationships for them. I pray for all the things I want for my own life. After praying *for* them, I find it's my heart that changes. The shackles of resentment release me from the bondage of anger and bitterness.

In some situations, forgiveness seems impossible, but it is never unattainable with God. We need to pray and ask for the power that's beyond ourselves to forgive. We have read countless stories of courageous people offering forgiveness, such as Corrie ten Boom, Sabina Wurmbrand, and Louis Zamperini. These people were able to forgive horrendous sins against them. God can empower you and me to do the same for those who have wronged us, including our spouse.

When our spouse wrongs us, it may help us to shift our perspective and view division — not our spouse — as the enemy. The wounding action that caused the division — the lie, the snide remark, the cut to the heart — that's the true enemy. Spouses must work together to defeat the true enemy: division and disunity. Forgiveness is easier with this mindset.

Imagine yourself having compassion for someone and doing them a special favor. Now imagine their response is to spit in your face and slap you *while you are completing* this act of kindness. Sickening, right? This is exactly what happened to Jesus. In Matthew 26, we read Jesus surrendered himself to be put on trial for a death that was not deserved. Not by him anyway. It was our death he signed up for. While he was on trial — voluntarily — his face was spat in and took a punch. Even still, he chose the cross for them. For us. His love was unwavering, as should be our love for others. We are never more like

Jesus than when we forgive. We have this incredible power to do the unthinkable — to forgive — within us.

When forgiving requires a power beyond the bounds of our capability, it is a powerful way to shine a light in a dark world. When people see our complete surrender of vengeance, they see God.

Discuss It: Are there any areas of unforgiveness in your life? Consider your extended family, friendships (past and present), church relationships, social media interactions, coworkers, and marriage. Now shift your focus to the real enemy, disunity. Take the blame off the person who wronged you and place it on their hurtful words or actions. Release the grip animosity has on you. Pray *for* the person.

Pray Over It: God, we thank you for offering forgiveness to us. We didn't deserve what you did for us. And you didn't deserve our death. Nor did you deserve to be spat on, punched, mocked, lashed, beaten, and hanged. We want to extend forgiveness to others as you have forgiven us. Reveal to us any areas of unforgiveness. Help us to tap into your power to forgive them. Though we've been hurt, we won't let it imprison us. [If you feel led, take time to ask God to bless in specific ways those who have wronged you.] Amen.

MARCH

LEAVE AND CLEAVE

*Therefore shall a man leave his father and his mother, and
shall cleave unto his wife: and they shall be one flesh.*

GENESIS 2:24 (KJV)

Within the account of Creation is the launching of the first marriage between Adam and Eve. As God was setting the stage for Biblical marriage, his instructions were for a man to leave his father and mother, cleave to his wife, and become one flesh with her.

God says to leave our father and mother. The bond between a parent and child is beautiful and essential. It has a specific purpose and is for only a limited timeframe. It is temporary. When we marry, that bond then transfers to someone else—our spouse—permanently.

In ancient times, it was highly valued to show honor and devotion to one's parents. Not only does our current culture need more of that, but the Bible commands us to honor our parents and not curse them (Exodus 20:12, Proverbs 20:20). To leave our parents doesn't mean we don't take care of them or respect them. We should, in fact, continue to value them, hold them in high regard, and ensure their care. But, to "leave and cleave" is to transfer loyalties from our parents to our spouse. This means our spouse becomes our priority. Honoring both our spouse and our parents is important, but if there comes to be a choice—listening to our spouse or listening to our mama, we listen to our spouse. If taking care of our parents leaves our spouse feeling neglected, we choose our spouse.

We leave our parents financially. This means we provide for one another independently from them. There is something about learning to make it financially together, especially when there is a struggle to overcome, that brings strength to a marital bond. An occasional gift from our parents may be okay to accept, but constant and consistent financial support is not leaving and cleaving. When the occasional gift from a parent is accepted, it cannot come with strings attached or manipulative statements like, "We gave you $2,000 and you won't spend Christmas with us on Christmas day…"

We leave our parents emotionally. If we need to talk to our parents to soothe our negative emotions, that is a red flag. If we need their encouragement to feel confident and secure — red flag. If we find that our parents put us on a guilt-trip to control us — red flag. If we blame them for who we are today, it's time to let go, forgive, rise up, and take responsibility for the kind of person we want to be from now on. Firm, clear boundaries may need to be put in place — both between us and our parents and, also, within our own heart.

We protect our marriage from parental interference. This means we don't run to our parents and bad-mouth our spouse when we have a conflict at home. This behavior sets our spouse up for animosity with our parents. It's the opposite of "leaving and cleaving." We need to solve the problem directly with our spouse (and involve a counselor, if needed) without involving our parents. We need to protect our spouse's reputation, allowing our parents to see him or her with pure affection, untainted by our personal conflict. This is crucial for a healthy, new family foundation.

We learn about relationships from our parents — how they resolved conflict, what they valued, and how they treated each other or dealt with their significant other. Naturally, we follow the patterns we witnessed growing up. It's easy to bring our past into our present. Sometimes, this is a great thing! However, most of the time, there are at least a few unhealthy habits we each bring into our marriage. We need to have awareness of these and decide which habits were healthy and beneficial and which were unhealthy and destructive. Then, we must work toward leaving behind the destructive habits, while keeping the productive.

Our parents are not the only ones who can come between us. We need to be guarded from anyone coming between us and our spouse. Jesus refers to this "leave and cleave" verse and then adds, "What God has joined together, let no one separate" (Matthew 19:5-6). Anyone who may be trying to get us to view our spouse in a negative light, anyone putting a wedge between us and our spouse, is bad news and needs introduced to a strong boundary.

We are to cleave to one another. The Hebrew word for *cleave* is *dabaq,* which means to cling like glue, to stay close to, and to mend any rifts. The verse goes on to say the two become one. When we are joined in marriage, we, as individuals, become one, as a team. Anything separating us as a couple must stop. People aren't the only ones separating us. Things, situations, and dilemmas do too. Our *individual* rights and concerns become null and are replaced by *our* rights and concerns, as a couple. Any independent desires should run through this filter: *How will this affect my spouse and my marriage?*

Before we married, we could have been a workaholic if we wanted. We could have spent hours of our free time solely on our hobby. It didn't affect anyone. Now, someone is affected—and that someone is our priority. Our spouse is at the top (just under God). Everything else—our job, our hobby, our friends, our family, our parents—surrenders to our spouse.

Discuss It: Are there any red flags in your relationship regarding your parents? Consider your parents' relationship habits. What was healthy and what was unhealthy? How can you be more intentional about leaving behind the unhealthy? Is there anyone trying to divide you as a couple? What healthy boundaries could you set in place? How could you make those boundaries clear to them? Have you made selfish decisions that negatively impacted your spouse? Is there anything you are allowing to take priority over your spouse?

Pray Over It: Father, since you are the creator of marriage, may we look only to you for guidance on how to leave and cleave. Give us awareness when we bring our past into our marriage. Give us wisdom in replacing the negative with positive. Forgive us when we have allowed anyone or anything to interfere with our marriage bond. Keep us glued together tightly. Help us to quickly mend any rifts. May we always choose one another above everything else. Amen.

THE LEASH OF FEAR

*For God gave us a spirit not of fear but of
power and love and self-control.*

2 TIMOTHY 1:7 ESV

Fear is a powerful tool of the enemy. It comes in many varieties
and each of us allows at least one type of fear to cripple us, such
as the fear of: not being good enough, being judged by others, failure,
disease, death, divorce, terrorism, the economy, losing a job, poverty,
criticism, losing control, rejection, pain… The list goes on.

Fear keeps us tethered to a pole when we were meant to fly. It
stalks us, always lurking in the shadows, waiting for the right time
to pounce. More often than not, fear attacks when God is about to
use us in a powerful way. Coincidence? Nope! The enemy pulls out
all the stops to hinder what God is about to do in, and through, us.

Timothy was young and timid. When Paul wrote this letter to
him, he did so to embolden him to continue ministry in Ephesus.
And where was Paul when he wrote this letter? Prison — facing his
death. He wasn't sitting in his jail cell freaking out or looming over
his impending doom. He was praising God, thanking God, trusting
God, and writing letters to encourage other people! Who does that?
Someone empowered by a Spirit not his own. Someone who does
not allow the enemy to use fear to cripple him.

Think about the possibilities, opportunities, and callings in your life
that may have been stonewalled by fear. Maybe it was venturing out into
a different career, volunteering where there's need, allowing friends into
your life, allowing your kids to experience things in which God intends
to use to build them up but you're too scared to let go, talking to someone about your faith, joining a small group that will challenge you?

Marriage and the depth to which spouses can connect is sometimes stunted by a specific kind of fear—fear of vulnerability and opening-up, fully, to one another. Maybe we're afraid of rejection, especially if we show our true selves. Maybe we fear judgement. Maybe we fear we'll be manipulated if we allow ourselves to be vulnerable. However, we can't be deeply loved without some level of vulnerability. In addition, building walls to keep our spouse from getting too close is a marriage killer. We might keep our *self* from hurt, but we keep *two people* from enjoying the emotional benefits of marriage. We deprive our spouse from having what he or she signed up for: emotional connection. Our spouse shouldn't be going somewhere else to get that, so shouldn't we be sure to provide it?

God's intention for marriage is for two people to come together, to be naked with one another and to feel no shame (Genesis 2:25). That means physically naked and emotionally naked. If you have had insecurities and difficulty opening up, here are some steps to move in that direction:

- When your spouse asks you a question, don't simply give short answers, such as "fine" or "no." Give details.

- Express your feelings about your day, about situations around you, about your spouse, about everything. Don't simply share your opinions, which are easy to tout out. Share your *feelings*.

- When your feelings are negative, refuse to "shut down." Instead, talk through them.

- Don't hide your imperfections. None of us are perfect. Join the club.

- Be open about your past and the fears triggering you to shut down.

- If crying in the presence of others makes you uncomfortable, tell your spouse how you want him or her to respond if you do cry. If the tears come knocking, allow them to fall along with the walls keeping you from a deeper level of intimacy.

- If it all seems too overwhelming, start small and work your way toward more.

Another fear that stunts our marriage connection is the fear of rejection regarding our physical body. We may not realize our negative body image has been impacting our sexual intimacy—keeping it shallow or non-existent. Body image strongly correlates to what we're willing to try sexually and can distract us from pleasure. Letting go of this fear can give both spouses greater sexual satisfaction. Perhaps counseling for body image is a necessary step.

Whatever fear is keeping you from fully connecting and enjoying each other, whether it be emotional or physical vulnerability, it may be time to deepen trust and jump in with both feet.

Discuss It: Get emotionally naked right now. Discuss fears you face outside of marriage. What silly, irrational fear do you have? What is a deep, disabling fear you have? In what ways has this fear crippled you? If fear were not in the picture, how would your life be different? Do you find it hard to open up to your spouse? Discuss how you would like your spouse to respond to your emotional vulnerability. Discuss your triggers with your spouse—the root of them, how they may have developed, and how you might overcome these fears.

Pray Over It: Powerful God, thank you for so generously giving us power over our fears. Thank you for giving us the gift of this marriage—a safe place to be naked and feel no shame. Please release any fears we may have. Help us to remember we do, indeed, have power over even *that* fear. We ask that, in all circumstances, you would give us peace despite our fears. May we treat each other's vulnerability with the respect it deserves. As our walls fall, may we fall in love more deeply with one another. Amen.

DESIGNED FOR INTERDEPENDENCE

*Carry each other's burdens, and in this way
you will fulfill the law of Christ.*

GALATIANS 6:2

I love the saying, "Not my circus. Not my monkeys." It's freeing to think another person's drama is not our own. However, the heartaches and suffering of other people and their tragic circumstances *are* our circus and those people *are* our monkeys. God's Word instructs us to die to "self" and take on the burdens of others alongside them.

We live in a culture of selfishness. Self-care is highly promoted. While taking care of oneself is a good thing, it becomes problematic when we are caught in self-absorption and fail to care about the burdens of others. Worse yet, we fail to even *notice* the heartache that surrounds us. This is the "me first" mentality. If it's inconvenient or doesn't serve a purpose, if it interferes with my peace or is uncomfortable, if there's nothing in it for me, or if it doesn't bring joy, pay it no heed for it's not my circus. However, that's not the way God created us to live.

We were not designed to be completely self-reliant. Movies like *Cast Away* and *Into the Wild*, show us the damaging effects of self-reliance. Scripture teaches us another way. It tells us to "carry each other's burdens." The Greek word for *burden* is *baros,* which conveys a weight that is heavy or crushing. Have you ever felt that way? Have you felt like you've carried a weight so heavy, you could fall under it and be crushed? When someone is under a pressing weight, it is the responsibility of others to stoop into that burden and carry it with them. Yes, we get messy. Yes, it's hard work. Yes, it is inconvenient.

Yes, it may require all the strength we have to lift it but lift it together we must. That is our calling.

Power lifters need someone to spot them—a buddy they can trust—to avoid being crushed in the process of bench pressing. Marriages are, in many ways, this type of spotting system. We should never stand by and watch, or turn a blind eye, as our spouse struggles. We are to lift the burden as much as possible. If it's not possible to completely remove our spouse's burdens, we can at least pick up our spouse, fill them with encouragement, jump into their struggle with them, and experience the burden alongside them. Carrying one another's burdens is powerful fuel for a great marriage! Marriage can double our joy and, if we carry each other's burdens, it can also divide our sorrow.

Since you and your spouse are one, if you lift your spouse, you, too, get to enjoy the upward flight.

Discuss It: Regarding relationships outside of marriage, on a scale with *self-reliance* on one end and *depending on others for help* on the other, toward which side do you lean? What keeps you from helping others? Think of a time you felt a crushing burden until someone came alongside you and helped you. Where would you be if they hadn't? Think of a time your spouse lifted a burden from you. Thank him or her for it. Consider the burdens that are currently crushing your spouse. Contemplate ways to lift it. If it is not possible, think of ways to encourage your spouse through it.

Pray Over It: Thank you, God, for not setting us up for failure due to complete self-reliance. Thank you for placing others in our lives that we might come to know the joy of bearing another's burdens. When we are tempted to believe we don't need others and when we are tempted to believe others brought on their own problems and, therefore, should carry their burden alone, please forgive us and change us. Teach us to live in community as you have established. In our marriage, help us to notice when the other is struggling with a burden. We pray you would give us the desire, ideas, and ability to lift one another's burdens. May we never take one another for granted. Amen.

HOW TO CARRY THE BURDENS OF OTHERS

*Carry each other's burdens, and in this way
you will fulfill the law of Christ.*

GALATIANS 6:2

God created people with a craving for purpose. Without purpose, we are more likely to suffer depression. According to *Journal of Medical Psychology*, research shows striving to help others and making a positive difference in others' lives improves depression.[3] So, in a way, helping others is a form of self-care!

Serving others gets our minds off our own perils for a bit to focus on someone else. Sometimes, when we step in to help others bear their crushing burdens, our own burdens come into proper perspective. We may realize our own troubles are not as crushing as we had imagined.

Sometimes perspective does no good because our burden truly is bigger than another's, but it's refreshing to take a break from our own and focus on another's. When I (Mandy) was going through cancer treatments, the focus was on *my* problem for such a long time. It was refreshing to go to the house of a mutual friend, who knew nothing of my problem, and pray with her over her special-needs child and brainstorm with her how to set up her house in a way to meet his needs. Unless we are unconscious, we can help another through encouragement and prayer. We can't minimize the power they hold.

Everyone we meet is carrying a burden. All around us people deal with divorce, eviction, disease, addictions, poverty, broken friendships, job loss, rebellious children, parenting a child who is bullied or has a disability, the loss of a loved one, watching a loved one suffer, being lied about to others, clinical depression, mental illness, or loneliness.

Sometimes, we feel compassion for others and want to help but don't know what to do. Often, in our inability to see how to help, we do nothing. How can we show up for others and lift their burdens? Approaches are endless. Here are a few ideas: landscape for the single mom, pack up the house for someone going through a divorce, give a financial donation to those having trouble paying bills, babysit or mentor a friend's kids, run to the store for a friend who is struggling to keep up or confined to the house (usually they will say they don't need anything, so word it like this, "I'm going to the store. Send me a list of some things you need."), send encouraging texts throughout the day, make a meal, take them a care package, give a long hug, take a pick-me-up treat to their work or home, take them out to talk, or just be present for them. Sometimes simply our presence, even in silence, is enough.

When I was going through cancer treatment, Joel's favorite way of feeling supported by others was not when others asked how he was doing. Talking about it over and over was exhausting. He said the best thing someone could do for him during that emotionally overwhelming time was simply to hug him and move on, requiring nothing from him. He also said the simple statement, *I'm praying for you,* reached deeper than others knew.

Here are a few dos and don'ts of carrying others' burdens: Don't give unwelcomed advice. It can come across as judgmental. Don't say you understand how they feel when you really don't. No two crises are alike—every burden is unique. You may have experienced a similar situation and have helpful and encouraging words; however, others may feel like you are just trying to "top" their situation. Although sharing may give them hope, don't *monopolize* the conversation with your similar experience. This makes it all about you when it's not. Be sensitive to the situation and to the other person's feelings. Ask God to help you be sensitive to whether advice is desired or obnoxious. Ask the other person, "Do you want to know about my experience with this? Or do you just want me to listen?" Don't say things like, "I'm here if you ever need me," or "Please let me know if there's anything I can do." These are empty offers. It puts the ball in their court while you feel you "covered" it. A person in dire need is not going to call and ask for help. Their need is so great, it is all they can see. It's like expecting someone who has just fallen and hit the pavement to call 911 themselves and tell the paramedics how to treat them. Lastly, follow-up is essential. Mark it on your calendar to check up on them in the near future.

Praying for others is powerful and is commanded in Scripture. Knowing someone cares enough to pray for us can lighten some of the load. However, solely praying for them can become an excuse to stay out of their mess. *If I tell you I'm praying for you, then I don't have to show up for you.* Pray diligently for them, and then show up for them too.

How can we lift heavy burdens from our spouse? Serve him. Do a chore she normally would do. Stand up for her when others put her down. Build him up through encouragement. Offer long hugs. Express gratitude for her. Support his dreams. Make that difficult phone call for her (We're not saying make the call in a situation in which you aren't involved like the conversation with her boss to quit her job, but calls either of you can be involved, like the call to the school regarding your child or with the family to define a boundary you have made). Create time to listen to her—listen with compassion and without interjecting advice (unless your spouse wants advice). Release his tension through massage or sexual intimacy. Pray for one another.

Just as lifting weights makes us physically stronger, lifting burdens from one another makes our marriage stronger.

Discuss It: Who do you know, outside your marriage, that is carrying a heavy burden? In what way can you lift that burden with them? Put it in your calendar right now. Share with your spouse a current burden you carry. Brainstorm together practical ways to lift those burdens from one another.

Pray Over It: Father, thank you for those in our community who have been there to lift burdens from us [list them out]. Help us to be sensitive to others' needs outside our marriage, to be able to see through the masks they wear, into their deep needs. Give us the time, wisdom, and energy to help others and give us insight into how we can lift their burdens. Thank you for giving us one another. Help us to see when the other is struggling and give us ideas on how to lift each other's burdens. Amen.

APRIL

GETTING WHAT YOU ASK FOR

You desire but do not have, so you kill. You covet but you cannot get what you want, so you quarrel and fight. You do not have because you do not ask God. When you ask, you do not receive, because you ask with wrong motives, that you may spend what you get on your pleasures.

JAMES 4:2-3

Y ou do not have because you do not ask God." WOW—that's great news! We want; we ask! But how many times have we, for our own benefit, taken this out of context? Sometimes we take this to mean we can have whatever we want, if only we ask for it. If we read further, we learn there are conditions of the heart that are prerequisites for receiving what we ask for.

You might appreciate the way *The Message* puts this verse: "You wouldn't think of just asking God for it, would you? And why not? Because you know you'd be asking for what you have no right to. You're spoiled children, each wanting your own way." We've got a double problem. First, we are by nature selfish and second, we don't see the big picture. Combine the two and BAM! That's why we "do not have." We want what we want without awareness of the grand scheme, and we want it with concern only for ourselves. Instead of trusting God to work things out for our good, we try to control God, reducing the Almighty Creator of the universe to a vending machine. We pop in the dollar prayer, push the button of our desire, and wait for the ordered blessing to drop down. When the blessing doesn't drop down, we pound our fists and curse the illusory vending machine.

"When you ask, you do not receive, because you ask with wrong motives, that you may spend what you get on your pleasures." What are we pursuing? Is it the will of God? Or is it our own personal desire for our own personal pleasures? Our desire for self-serving pleasures begins to erode our prayer lives. We do not get what we want because we are asking, "My pleasures be bestowed upon me," rather than, "Your will be done."

God *wants* to give us wonderful gifts (Psalm 31:19). When we align our prayers with what God truly intended for us, he gives us what we ask. However, when we don't receive what we ask for, it's because his desires for our lives are different than our desires. Sometimes it feels like God has it out for us when a barrage of tragic situations crashes down on us, one after the other. The truth is, God does have our best interest in mind, and he wants us to trust that truth. But to receive from the Lord, we must give up authority over what is best and give God free reign. When we submit and obey, we realize what we thought we wanted has no value in comparison to the true gift God wants to give when we surrender.

When we come to know him better, we come to know what to ask for. God hears and answers prayers that are pure, based on his promises, and free of our selfish desires. When we ask according to his will, which we can know by reading his Word, we will receive his perfect gifts in his perfect timing, not ours. An example was set for us by Jesus. The night before his horrifically pain-filled crucifixion, Jesus prayed in that darkest time for the hardest thing: "Yet, not what I want, but what you want" (Mark 14:36 GNT).

So, what can we pray for? Can we pray for a new car, to climb the corporate ladder, and for our favorite sport's team to win? Sure! We can pray for whatever we want, but if it's not promised to us, we can't take it to the bank. There are many promises we *can* bank on. Basing our prayers on these Scriptures, we can have confidence we will receive what we ask for when his timing is right. Here is a list of promises we can pray with confidence that we'll receive:

God Will Fight For Us. "The LORD will fight for you; you need only to be still" (Exodus 14:14).

Strength. "He gives strength to the weary and increases the power of the weak" (Isaiah 40:29).

Renewed Strength. "...but those who hope in the LORD will renew their strength. They will soar on wings like eagles; they will run and not grow weary, they will walk and not be faint" (Isaiah 40:31).

Help & Support. "So do not fear, for I am with you; do not be dismayed, for I am your God. I will strengthen you and help you; I will uphold you with my righteous right hand" (Isaiah 41:10).

Wisdom. "If any of you lacks wisdom, you should ask God, who gives generously to all without finding fault, and it will be given to you" (James 1:5).

Forgiveness. "If we confess our sins, he is faithful and just and will forgive us our sins and to purify us from all unrighteousness" (1 John 1:9).

God's Presence. "The LORD himself goes before you and will be with you; he will never leave you nor forsake you. Do not be afraid; do not be discouraged" (Deuteronomy 31:8).

Provision of Needs. "And my God will meet all your needs according to the riches of his glory in Christ Jesus" (Philippians 4:19).

Comfort. "Even though I walk through the darkest valley, I will fear no evil, for you are with me; your rod and your staff, they comfort me" (Psalm 23:4).

Forgiveness & Love. "You, Lord, are forgiving and good, abounding in love to all who call to you" (Psalm 86:5).

Freedom From Fear. "The LORD is my light and my salvation—whom shall I fear? The LORD is the stronghold of my life—of whom shall I be afraid?" (Psalm 27:1).

To Walk in the Light. "I am the light of the world. Whoever follows me will never walk in darkness, but will have the light of life" (John 8:12).

A Full Life. "The thief comes only to steal and kill and destroy; I have come that they may have life, and have it to the full" (John 10:10).

A Fruitful Life. "I am the vine; you are the branches. If you remain in me and I in you, you will bear much fruit; apart from me you can do nothing" (John 15:5).

Honorable Qualities. "But the fruit of the Spirit is love, joy, peace, forebearance, kindness, goodness, faithfulness, gentleness and self-control. Against such things there is no law" (Galatians 5:22-23).

Peace. "Peace I leave with you; my peace I give you. I do not give to you as the world gives. Do not let your hearts be troubled and do not be afraid" (John 14:27), and "You will keep in perfect peace those whose minds are steadfast, because they trust in you" (Isaiah 26:3).

Reward for Kindness to Enemies. "If your enemy is hungry, give him food to eat; if he is thirsty, give him water to drink. In doing this, you will heap burning coals on his head, and the LORD will reward you" (Proverbs 25:21-22).

Direction. "Trust in the LORD with all your heart and lean not on your own understanding; in all your ways submit to him, and he will make your paths straight" (Proverbs 3:5-6).

Adoption Into God's Family. "Yet to all who did receive him, to those who believed in his name, he gave the right to become children of God" (John 1:12).

To Overcome the World. "For everyone born of God overcomes the world. This is the victory that has overcome the world, even our faith" (1 John 5:4).

Freedom From Sin. "For sin shall no longer be your master, because you are not under the law, but under grace" (Romans 6:14).

Power Over the Enemy. "Submit yourselves, then, to God. Resist the devil, and he will flee from you" (James 4:7).

Power, Ability to Love, Self-Control. "For the Spirit God gave us does not make us timid, but gives us power, love and self-discipline" (2 Timothy 1:7).

A Transformed Life. "Therefore, if anyone is in Christ, the new creation has come: The old has gone, the new is here!" (2 Corinthians 5:17).

Joy. "Those who sow with tears will reap with songs of joy. Those who go out weeping, carrying seed to sow, will return with songs of joy, carrying sheaves with them" (Psalm 126:5-6).

Healing From Brokenness. "He heals the brokenhearted and binds up their wounds" (Psalm 147:3).

Relief From Grief. "So with you: Now is your time of grief, but I will see you again and you will rejoice, and no one will take away your joy" (John 16:22).

Mercy & Grace. "For we do not have a high priest who is unable to empathize with our weaknesses, but we have one who has been tempted in every way, just as we are—yet he did not sin. Let us then approach God's throne of grace with confidence, so that we may receive mercy and find grace to help us in our time of need" (Hebrews 4:15-16).

What if we know God's will, but it involves another person? People were given freewill by God—the choice to follow his ways or to reject them. Therefore, the effectiveness of our prayers that others would change is limited by the willingness of that person. Though God will not change someone against their will, God will provide us with what we need to get through circumstances regarding that person—peace, wisdom, strength. And in some cases, when we ask God to change someone else, we find he changes us.

Focusing on these promises of God will change your life. We encourage you to take one promise at a time and pray it regularly and faithfully, fully expecting to receive it because God's promises never fail.

There have been times I (Joel) was stuck in a no-win situation, and I didn't even know what solution to pray for. So, I simply prayed for God to move in that situation, open-endedly. It was mind-blowing to see how God worked it out. I can't look at a beautiful sunset or a mountain landscape and think, *This God doesn't want to show off what he can do.* God always comes through, but many times in expected ways.

Discuss It: What is the "silliest" thing you've ever prayed for? What was your motive? Did you receive it? If so, did it fulfill you? Think of a time God gave you what you *needed* instead of what you *asked* for. What have you recently been setting your heart on? Are your motives for this longing self-serving or Kingdom-serving? Look through the list of promises above. What promise speaks to your heart right now? What promise would most benefit your marriage?

Assignment: Pray three promises every day this week—the one you chose to pray over your life, the one your spouse chose over his or her life, and the one you've chosen for your marriage. Make a reminder for yourself—sticky note, phone alarm, ink on your hand—to pray these specific promises throughout the day.

Pray Over It: Giver of every perfect gift, thank you that the desire of your heart for us is good. Sometimes we want things that serve us only, not realizing what's best. We don't have the whole picture, a strong love for all people, everyone's best interest in mind, and pure-as-white motives as you do. Help us to keep our minds focused on your will in all things. We pray our desires would be for the right things with pure, unselfish motives. Thank you that your Word is clear, your promises are true, your gifts are perfect, and we can expect them in your perfect timing when we ask for them. Amen.

DECEITFUL DESIRES OF OLD SELF

You were taught, with regard to your former way of life, to put off your old self, which is being corrupted by its deceitful desires; to be made new in the attitude of your minds; and to put on the new self, created to be like God in true righteousness and holiness.

Ephesians 4:22-24

When someone drowns, their lungs fill with water, preventing breathing. The water must be forced out of their lungs to make room for air. In a spiritual sense, our "old self," defined in our verse as our "former way of life," has been drowning us, choking the life out of us. As in physical drowning, the end result of spiritual drowning is death—death to the soul, death to abundant life. Our "former way of life" prevents us from inhaling the air we were designed to breathe, which is the very Spirit of our Creator who gives life in abundance (Genesis 2:7, Job 33:4).

When we're drowning in "deceitful desires," we don't always realize. These desires come natural to us and blend in perfectly with our cultural norm. Therefore, it takes being in the Word to run point-blank into the "old self" with a clear picture of what a "new self" should look like (Hebrews 4:12). When solving a multi-step math problem, if everything is correct except one little step, the whole answer will be wrong. Worldly thinking, our old self, is much the same. There is a great deal of truth in the world's reasoning, but it is interwoven with error and unless we're going back to the Word to find truth, we won't be able to recognize those lies concealed in truth. The lies of the world that lead us to "deceitful desires."

Some examples of worldly "truth" that lead us to "deceitful desires" and end up choking us to death include thoughts such as: *I need more and more to be satisfied. It's fine to manipulate others to get what I want. I must step on others or lie to get to the top. It's okay to criticize others who do things differently than I do. It's not a big deal to treat others of a different race, gender, or religion with disrespect. Porn will gratify me and is a victimless crime. I can live above my level of income. I should retaliate against others who offend me to prevent myself from becoming a doormat. I can save face by blaming others when my own failures are brought to light.* This way of thinking points to a corrupted heart and is counter to what we were created to be. We think we're preserving and gratifying ourselves when, to the contrary, our souls are being corrupted—we're dying.

Corruption is a powerful word. When Paul says we are being corrupted by "old self ways," he is not painting a pretty picture. It's not something we can take lightly or skim over as he is not talking about socially unacceptable behavior, rather utter destruction of our souls.

There must be a change in our thinking. Our thoughts must be different than the rationality of the world, which is faulty, shadowed, and darkened with lies. The only way to recognize thoughts darkened by lies is to get a glimpse of the Light. Getting to know God will always change us. As we trust God as the final authority over right and wrong, our thoughts and attitudes change. We appear different than the world in both our actions and in the deep recesses of our hearts. It's not that our "new self" no longer has the thoughts and temptations of the "old self," but knowing and experiencing God brings awareness that the negative thoughts and temptations are a part of our "old self" and, in fact, are corrupting us. Recognizing them as "deceitful desires," we can avoid corruption by nailing our temptations to the cross and rising above with our "new self."

In a sense, marriage creates in us a "new self" as well. Before marriage, it was okay to spend all our spare money on our hobby, to devote all our spare time at the gym, and to watch TV at whatever volume we wanted at midnight. When we marry, we turn from our former way of life; we say goodbye to flying solo and so-long to looking out only for ourselves. Our "old self" was "me," but our "new self" is "us." We break up with bachelorhood to become fused allies, a team. If our desires benefit only ourselves while our spouse takes the short end of the stick, then those desires are "deceitful" and lead to the corruption of our marriage. The attitude of our minds must be made new to consider what is best for our "team."

Discuss It: Do any of the listed worldly "truths" stand out as something you've bought into believing would help you? Can you identify other deceitful desires that need to be "put off" as part of the old self? Consider any selfish desires that may be preventing your marriage from growing deeper. How would your marriage look different if you never considered "me" again, only "us"?

Pray Over It: God, thank you for your Word which enlightens us to that which drowns us and to that which brings us life abundantly. Teach us to recognize and put off our old selves daily. When our desires are simply self-serving, give us new desires for what is best for us spiritually, for each other, and for our marriage. Amen.

PUTTING ON THE NEW SELF

You were taught, with regard to your former way of life, to put off your old self, which is being corrupted by its deceitful desires; to be made new in the attitude of your minds; and to put on the new self, created to be like God in true righteousness and holiness.

EPHESIANS 4:22-24

There are some people who seem to merely exist. In a room full of people, they sit with arms-crossed and faces dead-panned, barely speaking a word. At home, they tune out the family, showing no interest in those around them. We've walked through journeys with a few of these people who then experienced life-altering events, shaking them to their core, causing them to awaken with a fresh passion and zeal for life. God worked behind-the-scenes to renovate their souls, turning the walking dead into the walking invigorated! After the Spirit awakened them, they came alive with passion for a world unseen to us. They began to feel joy for the first time ever. They felt a renewed enthusiasm for life and a new-found compassion for others. Not only did they feel the effects of the transformation, but it was also evident to everyone who knew them.

Some of us go through a dynamic transformation over a short period of time, while others experience changes on a smaller scale over a greater amount of time. Nevertheless, when we allow Christ the room to move in our hearts, we will change.

When we're made new by God's love and discipline, we become the person we were created to be. We produce the fruit of God's Spirit and are not governed by our selfish desires. Our "new self" reveals

God in all we do as we reflect him. We have new longings to love, convictions to choose righteousness, power to live free from guilt, strength to weather the storm, capacity to understand and demonstrate compassion, loving acceptance for people different from us, determination to remain faithful when nothing makes sense. In short, we are "being made new in the attitude of our minds." We are becoming that person who was "created to be like God in true righteousness and holiness."

We don't simply sign up with Jesus, then work hard to change our actions with our own little self-improvement plan — that is legalistic and futile. Change happens, by grace through faith, so God gets all the glory, not us. God creates the new person we are to "put on." For example, without God causing the change, our legalistic self-improvement agenda would simply be slapping a fake smile over hostility — basically putting a bandage on cancer. Our Creator is the only one who can transform a heart. If we will obey, he will transform.

God offers this gift of a "new self." We are welcome to waste it and leave it in the pretty gift package. But to take advantage of it, we are required to be participants in the action and put the "new self" on. It takes motivation. It takes discipline. It takes courage, prayer, and accountability. It takes being in the Word regularly. When driving without cruise control, we occasionally check our speed. If we make it a habit, every time we see a speed-limit sign, to glance down at our speed, we keep ourselves in check. In a spiritual sense, the Word of God is a speed limit sign we pass every day.

Lastly, we are called to righteousness and holiness. God cannot tolerate sin. God and sin are incompatible, like magnets that repel. Sin cannot exist in his presence. Therefore, this "old self" full of sin drives us away from God. When we are living in sin, we are separated from God's presence and cannot hear from him (Isaiah 59:2, Micah 3:4). We must show sin the door if we want the life-changing companionship of our Maker.

Jesus is serious about sin. In Matthew 5:30, he says, "And if your hand — even your stronger hand — causes you to sin, cut it off and throw it away. It is better for you to lose one part of your body than for your whole body to be thrown into hell." Though it would seem Jesus is into self-mutilation, he is using extreme, figurative speech to help us understand the criticality of the sin. He's saying, whatever is causing you to sin needs dealt with seriously — eliminated — even if it's as painful as losing your dominant hand. If you're tempted by a certain TV show, cancel the subscription to that show's platform. If the temptation is on your phone, install an accountability app. If you're prone to drunkenness, don't hang in the company of drunk friends. If you notice you're more prone to sin when you're with your friend, Jim, don't hang out with Jim or bring along another friend you know will encourage you to make the right choices. If you're tempted to have an affair on the job, transfer within the company or change jobs. Jesus is that serious about your purity, and he will honor your sacrifice. To be "made new" is not to be deprived of your desires but to have life to the fullest, life more abundantly.

The last part of this Scripture says we were created to be like God in true righteousness and holiness. Holiness is our destiny. Marriage is one of the many tools God uses to get us there. Here's how:

- Marriage sharpens us by forcing us out of our selfishness. We *cannot* be selfish and have a healthy marriage.

- When we become distracted from facts and logic, our spouse can remind us of the truth.

- A spouse can recognize things we didn't notice, such as sin creeping up on us.

- A spouse has a front row seat to our situations — a valuable, useful position — which means they can help us find the right way and encourage us as we move in that direction.

It's important to clarify it is not our job to "fix" our spouse. Sometimes, though we have good intentions, we nag or manipulate to move our spouse in certain directions. However, these behaviors only divide us as a team. We may be right. We may have the truth. Our perceptions might be extremely helpful to our spouse.

However, nagging only puts up their defenses and closes the door for them to receive our ideas and truth. How do we know when we've moved from helpful wisdom to nagging? How often are we mentioning it? Once is great. Twice may be okay. Beyond twice, we're nagging. By this time, our spouse knows our thoughts and we've moved from beneficial sharing to pressuring or controlling, which is only damaging.

Manipulation is detrimental as well. We are familiar with some of the obvious manipulation strategies like rewarding others through bribery or punishing them by withholding good from them. Commonly, in a marriage, manipulation comes in the form of withholding sex or giving the silent treatment. Many times, manipulation has been ingrained in us and we don't even notice we're doing it. Let's ask ourselves our intentions: *Am I acting this way to change the direction of another?* If the answer is, *yes*, we are manipulating. If we're not leaving room for another to make decisions that differ from our own, we are controlling. Rewards and punishments do not belong in a marriage.

Encourage your spouse toward holiness, to put on his or her "new self" without nagging or manipulating. This means, mention it, pray about it, and then give space. Allow God to change your spouse's heart in the way only God can. You will find sometimes it's your own heart God will change.

Accountability to put off the "old self" is important in a marriage, but it cannot fall completely on our spouse alone. He or she wasn't created to be everything. We all need someone, outside our marriage, checking in on us and holding us accountable. Sometimes our sin is causing our spouse pain. Sometimes, our struggle is an area our spouse cannot relate. Sometimes the best wisdom comes from an outside, unbiased resource. Meeting with a friend or mentor on a regular basis, weekly or monthly, is a grand opportunity to move into our "new self." Meeting with someone regularly is not solely about the struggles. Even during the good times, it's necessary to have someone, aside from our spouse, routinely pouring into our lives to achieve our best self.

Discuss It: Have you ever witnessed a soul transformation in either yourself or someone else? Practically speaking, how can you unwrap the packaging of your "new self" and put it on? What actions can you take to guard yourself from falling into the trap of deceitful desires? Don't accuse your spouse. Simply consider whether, in an attempt to get your spouse to put on their "new self," *you* have pressured, punished, bribed, nagged, or manipulated in any way. Consider offering an apology. If you're not currently meeting regularly with someone for accountability, who might be a good fit for this? Consider asking them to commit to meeting over coffee with you.

Pray Over It: God, thank you for making us new through what you have done. We're grateful you give us a new way of thinking. Help us to put to death the desires of our old selves and to live in the awareness of the new creation you offer. Help us to recognize in ourselves when we're nagging or manipulating. Give us strength to step back and give one another space to put on our new selves as you bring about the change in our hearts. Help us to find someone who will keep us accountable and help us put on this new self. Thank you for breathing into us the very breath of you which produces love, joy, peace, patience, kindness, goodness, faithfulness, and self-control. Amen.

A SUITABLE HELPER

The Lord God said, "It is not good for the man to be alone. I will make a helper suitable for him."

GENESIS 2:18

As we read in the account of creation, woman was created sequentially after man, but for what purpose? God created various features of the earth in stages. After each stage, he stated it was good—except for man. After creating man, God was not entirely pleased as he looked on man in his state of solitude, even surrounded by animals. Man, in his loneliness, needed someone "suitable" for him as the NIV puts it, or "comparable" to him as the NKJV puts it (Genesis 2:18). So, God created for man a comparable human, woman. The original Hebrew writing called her the *ezer kenegdo* for man. *Ezer* means "to give aid" and *kenegdo* means "corresponding to him" or "opposite him." This term is literally translated to mean "to give aid for him."

Let's dig further to gain insight into exactly what kind of aid woman was to give man. The Hebrew word *ezer*, "to give aid," is used in the Bible twenty-one times and sixteen of those times, the word *ezer* was used to reference God as the *ezer*, or rescuer, when the people desperately needed him to come through for them (Deuteronomy 33:7, Psalm 70:5, Psalm 121:1-2). Never was it used to describe a subservient position. Although woman was created second, she was not created *second-rate*.

The word *ezer* was often used to describe military aid during battle—vitally important, powerful acts of rescue and support. She was to be a warrior for him.

Kenegdo means "corresponding to him" or "opposite to him." We like the analogy Mikella Van Dyke from Chasing Sacred uses to help us understand what "opposite to him" looks like. She says, "A great visual explanation of the word *kenegdo* would be two wings on a bird, they are not the same, but are equal. They correspond to each other, both are useful for flight, but they are not identical. When both are used together, they accomplish one purpose—movement towards Christ. *Kenegdo* denotes the idea of equality, a mirror image of a man, but the opposite of him."[4] When both wings are used together in tandem, they accomplish one mighty purpose.

This beautiful design for the relationship between man and woman was in effect before the fall in the Garden of Eden when all was well and perfect in the world. Man and woman were managing God's creation together (Genesis 1:27-28). Imagine both you and your spouse managing your lives—family, careers, and all decisions—together. Both of you flapping your wings in harmony to move your team forward.

Harmonious teamwork was God's original design. But man and woman, together, ruined God's plan, bringing calamity to our perfect world. We now have a woman who longs for her husband and her husband rules over her—again, not the original plan (Genesis 3:16). The two are at odds with one another. Woman longs for equality with man—to have her opinions considered, to make as much money as a man for the same job, to make decisions for herself, and to not be overpowered by man.

Man overpowering woman was a part of the fall and is sinful—not God's intent. Though we have come far in righting this wrong, unfortunately, many parts of the world, and even some subcultures in America, are still operating with men crushing, oppressing, or dominating women. But keep in mind, God's original intent was for man and woman to run the show together. (This idea is not ignoring God's command in Ephesians 5:22 for a wife to submit to her husband. For clarification on a wife's role, read Appendix B.)

In a marriage, the friction between a husband and wife is due to the consequence of sin. All the behaviors that are detrimental to our marriage are due to living out this curse. How do we get back to the original intent of the relationship between man and woman? A man is not to "rule over" his woman. In fact, man is to cherish her, sacrifice for her, and give himself up for her (Ephesians 5:25). Nor is a woman to disrespect her man. A wife is "aid" to her husband. This means she is supporting him and cheering on his success. She is to have a gentle spirit and to be a safe place for him to find peace (1 Peter 3:1-4). She is to breathe life into him with encouragement and respect. Man and woman, having mutual respect for each other, sacrificing for each other, and cherishing each other, are the wings flapping in tandem to propel their team forward together.

Discuss It: Husbands, think of a time when your wife came to your aid or rescued you. Thank her for that. When have you, as husband and wife, accomplished a great deal while flapping your wings in tandem toward the same goal? In what way are you flapping in opposite directions? Discuss how you can move together in unity in this area.

Pray Over It: God, we thank you for your wonderful design for marriage. Please give us wisdom in our areas of disagreement so we could have a unified goal. May neither of us overpower the other but work together to meet the goals you placed in our hearts. Amen.

MAY

A HOUSE DIVIDED WILL FALL

If a house is divided against itself, that house cannot stand.

MARK 3:25

A house divided against itself cannot stand. When Jesus made this statement, he had been casting out demons from people. Teachers of the law were growing more and more suspicious of him. They accused Jesus of being possessed by Satan. Jesus's retort was that Satan would not drive out his own demons as they were on the same team, working toward the same goal!

Although this verse refers to Jesus and the illogical argument he was possessed by demons, it also makes a good point for marriage as we, also, are on the same team working toward the same goals. Unfortunately, our marriages don't often reflect this. When we marry, our goal is no longer self-preservation but team preservation. It's easy to forget this and return to our habit of self-preservation.

Our natural human instinct is to climb in rank to others. We want admiration. We want others to look up to us. Sometimes, we even talk down to others to get them to step down to the "inferior place" we have deemed them. We believe we're smarter, stronger, better at decisions, and have a better way of doing things. We keep a mental tally of all the things we did right, and all the things they did wrong. Then, we bring it up later to prove a point — *we are the better one.* To ascend, we undermine others without considering their feelings. If we bring this mentality into our marriage, we can watch the marriage dissolve.

Think about a sports team. Teammates communicate with each

other, plan their game collaboratively, coordinate their efforts, share the ball, pass to the teammate with the clear shot or to the one skilled enough to make the goal. They come to each other's defense. They push through cooperatively, until they've completed the task *together*.

What would it look like for you and your spouse to work together as a team? Envision your marriage this way—communicating with each other, planning your "game" collaboratively, coordinating your efforts, sharing the workload of the household chores, defending one another when attacked, respecting each other's feelings, appreciating the fact that your spouse does things differently, and being okay with that. Doesn't this sound like the perfect game plan?

Who is your favorite NFL quarterback? Though he does a good job in his quarterback position, imagine if the entire football team was made up of multiple clones of him. That team would be terrible! Consider the various strengths of each team member. The lineman and wide receiver require different skills and body types. The team functions best when the various strengths are all being used in their different positions.

Just as a team places people in positions based on their strengths, husbands and wives bring different strengths into the marriage. There's a reason opposites attract. Your differing natures may frustrate you, but they counterbalance your team, allowing you to achieve more together. One person may be good at budgeting, one may have superb organizational skills, one may be the dreamer imagining the impossible while the other has practical, strategical plans to bring the dream to reality. Together, the dream is accomplished.

You can divvy up the home responsibilities to the person with the strength in that area. But keep in mind, even though you may be stronger in a certain area, there are other things to consider. Maybe it's your spouse's passion. Maybe your spouse believes he or she has the strength in that area. Moving forward together as a team means more importance is placed on protecting your spouse's confidence and uplifting your spouse's spirit than "being right" or having the task done your way.

What if your house is divided because you and your spouse disagree about an issue? *Pray.* Many couples find if both spouses are praying about a decision, God gives them a peace about taking one direction over another. The answer doesn't always come right away. Keep at it. Continue asking God for unity in this decision. Talk about it with a pastor, a mentor, a counselor, or other couples who have demonstrated wise decision-making. Sometimes others can see more objectively without feelings distorting their view. Consider whether moving in one direction or the other spurs only one teammate forward while leaving the other in the dust. Ask yourself which way moves the whole marriage and family forward.

In a marriage, you *complete* each other, not *compete* with each other. You either win together or lose together. Philippians 2:3-4 says, "Do nothing out of selfish ambition or vain conceit. Rather, in humility value others above yourselves, not looking to your own interests but each of you to the interests of the others." Does your spouse feel like his or her best interest is your priority? Do you find it's unacceptable for your spouse to feel like a loser? Does your spouse feel like a winner? If so, *you* are winning!

Discuss It: Don't answer this first question aloud or accuse your spouse, simply give it thought. Have you been putting your spouse down to get them to view you as superior? Where have you been trying to compete (moving self forward) instead of trying to complete (moving team forward)? What are your spouse's strengths? In what areas could you and your spouse improve at working together? If there is a topic of disagreement, to whom could you go for objective advice?

Pray Over It: God, thank you for our diverse strengths. Sometimes the contrast brings difficulty to the marriage, but we pray we would learn to use these strengths to move our team forward instead of moving each of us forward individually. Please help us to see each other as teammates, not competitors. Remind us to show each other respect in all circumstances. Please guide us both in the same direction you want us to go so we will be unified as we move forward together. Amen.

UNWHOLESOME HEARTS

Do not let any unwholesome talk come out of your mouths,
but only what is helpful for building others up according
to their needs, that it may benefit those who listen.

Ephesians 4:29

What is "unwholesome talk"? Some think "unwholesome talk" is certain four-letter words. However, when we take the whole verse in context, it implies unwholesome talk as words that are destructive to others. Refraining from saying @#$&, yet attacking another's character, is no better than the hearts of the Pharisees, following their man-made laws and completely missing the spirit behind the command.

Unwholesome talk and destructive words: We're guilty of this. You're guilty of this. Every single one of us. We can be mean, especially to our spouse. We think mean things about them, judge them for doing things differently than we would, become impatient when they disagree, and hang on to bitterness when they mistreat us.

The mean words we speak begin with our thoughts. Though we try to hold in these thoughts, they slip out of our mouths and spread dark clouds over the family. Out they shoot—cruel and cutting words, orders barked, arguments, lies, put-downs, complaints, words that destroy the spirits and reputations of those we love.

God knows the damaging words come from an impure spirit—a spirit not fully surrendered, not seeing others through his eyes. If our minds and hearts are full of negativity, those thoughts will slip out and wound others. This is the reason God doesn't simply want us to bite our tongues, he wants sincere change in our hearts. When our hearts are surrendered, the wholesome talk follows.

We cannot change our hearts with our own strength. We can't simply make a decision to speak wholesomely from this day forward and BAM!—no more unwholesome talk. We need heart transformation only given through God. God assures us, "I will give you a new heart and put a new spirit in you; I will remove from you your heart of stone and give you a heart of flesh" (Ezekiel 36:26).

How do we get this "heart change" from God? Just as something that glows in the dark needs to be placed near a source of light to glow, so do our hearts. When we keep close to the light, we can glow in a dark world so desperately needing light (2 Corinthians 4:6, Matthew 5:14-16). After spending time in God's presence and soaking in his powerful light, we will glow, and our words will not be unwholesome and destructive, but build others up.

Let's consider the effect we have on our spouse and family. We have the power to make or break their day. When we take time to get our glow on, our relationships will have more harmony, life will become more positive and peaceful, we will find greater success at work, and we will prevent a heap of trouble in our lives. We have so much stuff to do and it's difficult to find the time, but we must be intentional about seeking God for a changed heart so we can get our glow on and light up, not only our homes, but the world!

Discuss It: Think about the words you have used in recent conversations with your spouse. How is the state of your heart lately? With which of these areas do you most struggle—insensitivity, impatience, barking at others, lying, putting others down, yelling at family members, prioritizing being "right" over having harmonious relationships, holding grudges, or complaining? Are there areas of your life that are not fully surrendered to the life changing power of God? Which area will you surrender today?

Pray Over It: Lord, God, please get our attention before destructive words leave our mouths. Transform our hearts. May we make room for time in your presence to get our glow on. May the thoughts and words coming from our hearts reflect love, gratitude, and positivity. May we see the best in others, have compassion and sensitivity, and replace harmful words with life-giving, wholesome words. Amen.

THE LIFE-GIVING POWER OF BUILDING ANOTHER UP

Do not let any unwholesome talk come out of your mouths,
but only what is helpful for building others up according
to their needs, that it may benefit those who listen.

Ephesians 4:29

To build physical strength, we lift weights. Likewise, the best exercise for our heart is lifting others up. Ironic how building up the hearts of others, in turn, elevates our own. Building others up is so important, Paul says we are to speak only for that purpose—only to benefit and build others up. Otherwise, we are not to speak!

What are some practical ways we can build others up?

- Choose to be kind, even when others have chosen otherwise.

- Offer grace. Although some people may deserve our piercing words, we are called to give undeserved favor—grace.

- Choose joy and spill it onto others who lack it.

- Express gratitude.

- Ensure our words come across in a gentle and loving tone.

- Encourage others.

Many times, we notice something admirable in another, but we just keep it to ourselves. You know those people whose facial expressions don't match what's going on in their head? That's me, Mandy. So often, Joel will ask me why I'm staring daggers at someone when I was just admiring their haircut! I'm trying to break this habit of keeping my positive thoughts to myself. (And I'm working on making my facial expressions match my thoughts and heart.) People don't know others see good in them until they are told. Joel didn't know I admired the way he could keep his cool with angry clients until I told him. I didn't know how much Joel loved my cooking until he communicated that to me.

Words have the power to bless or to break another. You have the power to blow the wind in someone's sail or to knock the wind out of it. Encouraging words are the fuel that keep each of us going.

Husbands and wives have incredible power over their spouse's self-image, dignity, and sense of worth. Use that power delicately and wisely. Of course, you want your spouse to feel as if he or she has value, but it's hard for them to feel of any value when they are constantly being torn down by their other half. When having a disagreement, try a different strategy. Don't try to "win" the argument, but instead, try to "win" the prize of self-worth for your spouse and his or her trust in you. Think about the topics you argue over, how you argue about them, and how you can "win" together. Sometimes, it's through gentle confrontation, allowing them to see your side in a considerate way. Sometimes it's keeping your mouth shut and praying. Sometimes, it's giving up on your own selfish way and allowing another way, even if it isn't the "best" way.

Children, especially, need our wholesome talk. When our children disappoint us, we sometimes let them get the best of us. We yell at them, scold them, or shame them because we expected so much more! These types of harsh reprimands could devastate their souls. While they do need correction, the lesson is better learned through consequences without the unwholesome, destructive words. Words easily wound a child's spirit, in some cases, for years to come. However, consequences calmy given cause them to think before acting the next time. It's the consequences that speak to their actions, and the destructive words that speak to their spirits. Children, more than anyone, need "helpful [words] for building [them] up according to their needs." They need us to catch them doing something right and give them frequent affirmation.

Let's touch base on another part of this Scripture that often gets lost: We are to build another up "according to their needs." We are all different in the way we receive another's words. Just as we can't put the same motor oil in a race car as we would put in a sedan, the way I would love to be encouraged may not go over as well by Joel. Something we might say with all good intentions might come across as hurtful to our spouse. Furthermore, we shouldn't pass off our spouse's pain just because we can't relate. We must be sensitive enough to find out their need along with their unique circumstance. By listening more and seeking to understand our spouse, we can learn how to build them up "according to their needs." Do they need a strong intervention or a gentle word of concern? Do they need more listening and less preaching? Do they need words of understanding or words of correction? God knows the specific needs of our spouse. So, first and foremost, it is imperative to seek God's direction in building them up "according to their needs."

Let's agree, no matter the circumstance, to spread love, joy, and peace through our life-giving words.

Discuss It: Make a mental note to be more intentional about letting others, especially your spouse, know when you notice something good in them. In what ways do you need to improve at building others up? Did you relate with unwholesome words directed at your kids? Or winning the argument with your spouse? Have you taken the time to seek God's direction with your words to meet the needs of others? Do you tend to pass off others' pain when you can't relate? How can you show compassion to others who have different sensitivities than you?

Pray Over It: Lord, God, sometimes we're more focused on the words we say than the spirit behind them. Help us to uplift others, no matter how angry they've made us, and no matter if our kind words are deserved. We don't deserve your grace, yet you pour it on us without limit. Help us to be like you. We pray we would be guided by sensitivity, even when we can't relate to one another's struggles. May our words build, rather than demolish, each other. Amen.

WORKING HEARTILY

*Whatever you do, do your work heartily, as for the
Lord and not for people, knowing that it is from
the Lord that you will receive the reward of the
inheritance. It is the Lord Christ whom you serve.*

COLOSSIANS 3:23-24 NASB

Sometimes we do a shoddy job with a half-hearted effort, depending on who the task is for and how we've been treated by them. We feel some don't deserve our wholehearted commitment after what they've put us through. This verse commands us to work "heartily as for the Lord"—not for people—and was written to the people in Colossae, many of whom were slaves. How hard it must have been for a slave stripped of freedom, dignity, and privileges, to work heartily for his master as if he was laboring for God himself. We are called to the same high standard.

The reason we are commissioned to work "as for the Lord," is not because he is dependent on us to do certain jobs. It's not about us meeting God's needs. It is about God meeting our needs. It's not uncommon for people to go to other countries for "missions work" to help the people there, but instead return home having been richly blessed and radically changed by the people whom they intended to serve. It's like that. When we work heartily as if for the Lord, God has a blessing for us that outweighs the work.

Let's think about this in the work setting. We may have no choice about our job responsibilities, our environment, or with whom we work, but we do have a choice whether we make it a pleasant experience for ourselves and the people around us. If we want to make it a positive experience, here are practical ways we can change our attitudes from resentful to hearty:

- Don't complain.
- Choose joy and laugh often.
- Be open to feedback.
- *Ask* for feedback.
- Don't cut corners.
- Choose kindness.
- Encourage others.
- Go the extra mile—even for people who don't deserve it.

Oftentimes, the quality of our work depends on how well we're being paid. If we're paid thirty dollars an hour to mow Mr. Smith's lawn, we tend to do a better job and pay better attention to details than we do with Mr. Anderson's lawn job that pays ten dollars an hour. Does your attitude on the job and quality of your work vary depending on the amount you're paid? Good news! God is generous and his pay scale is beyond our wildest dreams! Sometimes he provides us with earthly treasures. But *all the time,* he is depositing our pay into "an account" awaiting us in Heaven (Matthew 16:27). The reward God gives is more valuable than any paycheck, promotion, or accolades we'll receive here on earth and, best of all, it's insured and cannot be taken away. Sometimes we feel we're working hard for pennies while others who work minimum-effort jobs get the big bucks. Parenting is one of the most difficult duties on earth and pays absolutely nothing monetarily. But remember, though we may not be receiving a handsome pay for our work here, God is paying well, and he is asking us to do the job with *his* rate of pay in our hearts and on our minds. He calls for our best ability—not cutting corners, not complaining—but, working with absolute sincerity and devotion to the task. When we notice our attitudes taking a downward shift, let's take a deep breath and remember we're working for the best boss ever.

In addition to working heartily for the Lord, Christ expects us to lower ourselves to the position of a servant to others. Though Jesus was called the King of the Jews, he willingly took on the role of a slave when he washed the feet of his disciples. Washing feet was not an uncommon task in those days. In our time and culture, washing our neighbor's feet when they stop by would pose an awkward situation. But in that part of the world, the sand and wind mixed with a pair of sandals made for some dirty feet and it was common for guests to get a foot washing upon entering a home. That job was delegated to the slaves. It was a job others felt "above" doing. When Jesus washed the feet of the disciples, it was a radical statement, *Do what others feel they are too over-qualified, or too distinguished, to do and do it with sincerity.* There is no job too lowly, no person too great.

Now think about these teachings in the context of marriage. Maybe your spouse has been taking you for granted or has been rude and disrespectful. It was easy to serve them when they were putting their best foot forward but, lately, it has proved to be challenging. This is a sad state for a marriage—when one spouse serves while the other is rude and unappreciative—and the marriage can't grow here. But something else can grow—our relationship with God. He cherishes and honors our sacrifice as we serve our spouse heartily, as if for him, not for them.

I think of the movie *The Princess Bride.* From the very beginning of the movie, the farm boy, Westley, so in love, utters to Princess Buttercup whenever she asks him to do something (which she does often), "As you wish…" He was so in love with her, he would do anything for her, humbly and gratefully. It was through his actions and servant-like spirit he expressed his love for her. And so it should be for us, whenever we are tasked with anything. Loving God and committing our lives to him means our response to *his* request to serve our husband or wife heartily should be, "As You wish…"

Discuss It: What jobs bring out the worst in you? What jobs do you dread? What does it mean to you to work heartily as if for the Lord in your home, workplace, or place you volunteer? Have you ever been blessed more by those whom you intended to bless? Which of the above listed ways to change your attitude can you incorporate into your life? If you began doing all tasks "as for the Lord" rather than your employer, fellow volunteers, or family, what would you be doing differently? Are there any jobs you've felt should be left for others in a "lower position"? Consider doing these jobs with a humble and grateful attitude.

Pray Over It: God, please remind us that you require hearty effort, good quality, passion, and sincerity, in all that we do. We pray the attitude of our work is an accurate reflection of all you have done in our lives. Thank you for paying well and for the rewards that await us. Help us to remember that next time we're grumbling about our wages. Father, forgive us for the times we have thought we are better than others and have left some tasks to others that we could have done ourselves. Thank you, Jesus, for your attitude, humbly serving and showing us no one is too high and mighty. May our work be for you — a reflection of the lowly servant you became. We look forward to the day you return and say, "Well done, good and faithful servant." Amen.

JUNE

LOVE IS NOT DISHONORING OR SELF-SEEKING

It does not dishonor others, it is not self-seeking, it is not easily angered, it keeps no record of wrongs.

1 Corinthians 13:5

Love does not dishonor others. In Greek, the word for *dishonor* used in this verse means to be unseemly, rude, or not of good form or taste. It is discourteous, insensitive, cares little for the feelings of others, and flippantly disgraces another. We all know this person, and sometimes we *are* this person. Love is polite, courteous, and tactful. It is aware of the customs and traditions of others, showing high regard for people, not because we agree with their customs or traditions, but because we love and honor the person.

The second part of this verse says love is not self-seeking. The Greek word used here for *self-seeking* describes someone who insists, and even manipulates, to get his own way. To love without seeking our own way means something inside us must die, our will. We must be okay when things go someone else's way.

Maybe your spouse does things differently than you. Maybe he takes the longer route because he wants to avoid highways. Maybe she doesn't like to fill the tank until she's on the last drop of gas. Maybe he eats ice cream out of the container and then puts it back in the freezer with only one bite left. Maybe he loads the dishwasher the wrong way. Maybe she delays updating her phone until her phone shuts down. Maybe your spouse is doing life wrong, but that's okay.

It's not your job to dishonor, nitpick, and turn him or her to your way of thinking and doing things. It's your job to love and honor them, despite differences.

Here are practical ways to honor your spouse:

- Speak highly of him to others.

- Don't compare her to other wives.

- Praise the work he does.

- Show interest in her passions.

- Honor his decisions.

- Treat her—not as a servant—but as an equal.

- Build-up his character.

- Don't interrupt her.

- Keep a calm voice with him.

- Ask her about her day.

- Don't belittle him.

- Put her first before everything.

- Come to his rescue when he puts his foot in his mouth.

- Let her know you appreciate all the little things she does that usually go unnoticed.

- Don't go behind his back to do something you know he doesn't like.

- Ask her opinion before making decisions.

- Ask him before volunteering him to help others.

To not be dishonoring or self-seeking means we take genuine interest in others' points of view, cheer others on, give others credit where it's due, help others achieve their goals, sincerely desire others' success, and give them the freedom to do things their way. We support them, not because we agree with their method, but because we honor them as a person.

Discuss It: Have you said something to someone in a flippant or insensitive way? Consider apologizing for this. What does your spouse do differently than you? Take a moment to consider how you might honor your spouse despite this difference. Look at the list of practical ways we can honor our spouse. How could you better honor your husband or wife?

Pray Over It: God, thank you for teaching us, and showing us by example, what true love looks like. Help us to honor one another above ourselves. When we're only thinking of ourselves, help us to see and honor others because that's how we love like you. Amen.

LOVE IS NOT ANGRY OR BITTER

*It does not dishonor others, it is not self-seeking, it is
not easily angered, it keeps no record of wrongs.*

1 CORINTHIANS 13:5

ove is not easily angered. The Greek word for the phrase, *easily angered*, means to stimulate, to rouse to anger, or to be easily provoked. When we're easily angered, we're always ready to erupt. Others feel they must walk on eggshells around us because we're so easily offended. We go off like a bomb, leaving a ruined mess in our wake. It's hard to live with someone like this. We shouldn't expect our spouse to live on guard, never knowing when they'll feel the attack of our wrath. The deep trust we can only experience in a marriage can't be established when we're easily angered.

We all have buttons that trigger us, but some of us are a big, walking collection of buttons, even taking pride in the buttons, warning others not to bump the buttons. As love is not easily provoked, it has few buttons, and those buttons don't lead to explosions. As my peace-loving son says, "Be triggerless."

We all become angry at times—sometimes justifiably and sometimes not. However, habitual anger is often a sign of something deeper and is destructive to the soul. It can be a manifestation of depression or unresolved pain. Our anger may be—though unknown to us—misplaced. If you are a walking "collection of buttons," it might be time for some outside help from a counselor. There's no shame in getting counseling. We all need it at times. In fact, we—Joel and Mandy—have been to counseling for the same. When life gave us repeated lashings, we felt out-of-control and began snapping at each other for small things. Talking it out with a counselor helped. No shame in it!

The last part of our study verse says love keeps no record of wrongs. The Greek word for *keeps record* is an accounting term used to credit one's account. Like accountants, we tally the debits of others' wrongdoings, make a report in our hearts, and sometimes file a "statement" with the one who offended us. This is damaging to our health and prevents healing. Love doesn't bring up offenses after they've been settled, reminding others of the ways they've wronged us. Love doesn't "memory bomb" offenders to reinforce a point. Once settled, it's off the table. Reminding others of their mistakes is an ineffective, unproductive, and damaging way to resolve conflict and maintain relationships.

Gunnysacking is a common form of conflict resolution within a marriage—not healthy, but common. Gunnysacking is when someone silently stores up grievances in their "sack" until it becomes too heavy and they burst, pulling out all the resentment they had been storing up over time. An argument over one topic turns into a barrage of arguments. This technique is unhealthy as it distracts from resolving the current issue. If an issue needs addressed, address it by itself. Don't store it up in a sack to bring out later.

God chooses not to hold our sins against us (Psalm 103:10-12), and he requires us to do the same for others. Choose forgiveness. If you are the kind to journal and you've written down wrongs done to you, burn the journals. They are preventing your healing. Letting go of the journals is an outward sign of an inner letting go.

If your spouse has wronged you, it's okay to feel hurt. But you can't hang on to the hurt and allow a grudge to fuel the remainder of your marriage. The only thing that grudge will fuel is a giant chasm. That's no way to live. Decide you're not going to bring up the past wrong in future arguments. Let go of the grudge and allow the canyon dividing you to fill with forgiveness, mercy, and love. Allow your connection to grow deeper as you let go of the record of wrongs.

Discuss It: Are you one who is easily offended or "triggered"? If so, can you identify those areas where you may be overly sensitive? Has anger been a part of your daily life? If so, have you considered speaking to someone who can help you get behind your anger? Against whom have you been holding a grudge? No need to discuss this: simply consider any grudges you might be holding against your spouse. How can you release that record of wrongs?

Pray Over It: God, help us to be "triggerless." We guard our hearts to protect ourselves from pain, but we cheat ourselves of the deep connection marriage can give. Teach us to let go of our anger and our record of wrongs. Please protect our hearts as we open them. Only in your power can we do all this. Amen.

COMPLAINING

Do everything without complaining or arguing.

PHILIPPIANS 2:14

We are born crying. It takes six weeks until we show our first sign of delight—a smile! Complaining is deeply engrained in our human nature. It peaks during the "terrible twos." *Even though I threw a tantrum yesterday because I wanted applesauce, Mom should know that doesn't mean I like it today!* We eventually learn to control our outrage over these seemingly unjust situations. At about age four, most of us are beginning to learn some social norms. We notice other humans aren't throwing themselves to the ground in an award-winning display of drama because Mom said "no" to a donut for dinner. It's an uphill climb from there for us all. Even at age sixty-five, we're still squawking about trivial matters. Since grumbling is deep-seated within us, it takes conscious effort to overcome.

One would think people living on "Easy Street" would be joyful while those with bleak circumstances would be the grumbly ones. However, Americans are some of the most pampered people on earth, and surprisingly, the biggest whiners. We are entitled. We believe we deserve better and are worthy of so much more—and how dare others not "recognize"! On the other hand, in *all* the third-world countries we've visited, some of them for months at a time, we came to know some of the happiest, most grateful people. It doesn't seem circumstances affect our attitudes as we would expect.

Also, in America, political grumbling has reached its peak, and not just among politicians. Somehow, we think our arguing and grumbling is going to change minds and fix the world, but it only creates a deeper divide. Fierce conversations over the state of our world reveal hearts that don't trust God holds it all in his hands, that don't believe God sets up kings and takes them down (Daniel 2:21), or that God is as active in government today as he was in Moses's day when Pharaoh was at his mercy. It is possible to stay informed and involved politically while also putting our trust in God, even when things turn in the opposite direction than we think best.

Another popular arena for grumbling and arguing is social media. That is a swamp of negativity and endless complaining. We challenge you to a social media self-examination. To gain a perspective of your own attitude, look at the last twenty posts you have made. If most of your posts were negative, you may have a bigger problem with grumbling than you realized. If this is you, try withholding from the divisive conversations altogether and train yourself to do more listening (reading). When you do speak (post or comment), do it with understanding, respect, and humility.

Complaining is a sin, detestable to God (1 Corinthians 10:10, Numbers 11:1, James 5:9). It's one of the sins we often overlook. Most of the time, we don't even consider it a sin because we're all so prone to it. We think we're each entitled to a "grumpy day," or we can grumble because we "need to vent."

There's a difference between seeking advice through hard times and a spirit of complaining. Talking to someone about what we're going through and listening for another's advice is healthy. In fact, within a marriage, communication about *all* details — the good, the bad, and the ugly — is vital to a healthy relationship. While it is out of line to tell all who will listen for the sake of stirring them up against our offender, stating the problem to a trusted friend or family member in search of a solution is not in the spirit of complaining.

Our relationships will suffer when we choose a lifestyle of grumbling. We know we've become a problem when others, after spending time with us, need to go recharge alone or limit their time with us. Not only does grumbling affect those around us, but it has a monumental effect on the way we experience life. Maybe that's why God significantly despises complaining. It depletes the abundant life he wants to give us.

Though we should keep our spouse informed about everything, even the negative things going on in our life, we need to keep the complaining to informational purposes only. A *spirit* of grumbling is different—continuing to gripe about our situation even after we've informed our spouse or *looking* for the negative in everything—makes marriage difficult. It makes a spouse not want to be home. Nothing is attractive about someone who finds fault with everything. So, let's get rid of our complaining and allow our spouse to see the attractive side of our spirit.

To fight our chagrined spirits, first we need to become aware when we are complaining, then be intentional about changing gears. Bite back the complaints and, instead, seek God's hand in it, look for the positives in the situation, and offer the benefit of the doubt. Though we can't avoid disappointments, we can choose to what extent they will affect our lives. Is the problem all we can see? Or are we searching with hope for a way out? Are we pulling up a recliner, kicking up our feet, and settling into that dark pit of disgruntlement? Or are we refusing to dwell there and choosing gratitude instead? Are we spouting out unending negativity and self-pity, or are we discussing solutions to our problems?

Let's take the grievances to God in prayer, leave them at the Throne, and venture back into life with a renewed spirit.

Discuss It: Take some time right now to look at your past twenty posts. Do you tend to spout negativity or spread encouragement? What are you most prone to complain about? What positive things can you see in the situations you complain about? What effect has your grumbling had on the people who must listen to it? Do others need to go recharge alone after spending time with you? How can you hold yourself in check to change your thoughts?

Pray Over It: Father, we're sorry when we forget complaining is something you detest. We get comfortable with griping. We forget you require better from us. The next time a complaint comes to mind, help us to remember you can make beauty from ashes, and may we search for that beauty with expectation. Give us solutions and opportunities to rise above the things we complain about. We will be on the lookout for ways out of our problems even if it requires thinking outside the box. Amen.

GRUMBLES TO GRATITUDE

Do everything without complaining or arguing.

PHILIPPIANS 2:14

Joel loves all things history. So, when our family vacationed in Charleston, South Carolina, he was enthusiastic about scoping-out the many historical sites. History does not fascinate me in the same way. I wanted to spend our days relaxing on the beach and biking through town. Frankly, I *really* didn't want to waste time and feel bored on vacation. So, when we headed out to the plantation, I grumbled to the point Joel no longer wanted to go. I robbed him of what could have been an exciting day.

When I worked in a hospital, during *hospital week,* my employer would provide a lunch for its hundreds of employees to express their gratitude for our hard work. I was happy to not have to pack a lunch or buy food that week! However, I was soon brought down by some coworkers who were griping because they worked so hard and all they got for *hospital week* was a lunch. My cheerful mood was quickly brought down by the grumbling around me.

Complaining is contagious. Like a toxic disease, it works its way into our souls. It's too easy to join in with others kicking up a fuss. Not so easy to do the opposite and swim upstream. If our coworkers complain, our spouse complains, our friends complain, and we are reading a barrage of complaints on social media, we're bound to catch the disease. But here's the bright side—all emotions are contagious. Enthusiasm too! Have you ever attended an event that didn't interest you, but you unexpectedly had a great time because of the enthusiasm of those around you? If your emotions are going to transmit to others, what would you like others to catch?

Complaining literally affects brain and body function. A 2016 study by Stanford researchers found that complaining shrinks the hippocampus, which is the part of the brain critical to problem solving. This means our griping is limiting our ability to think a way out of our problems. In addition, complaining releases cortisol, the stress hormone, which raises the blood pressure and blood sugar. Frequent complaining can also lead to heart disease and diabetes. Those are some heavy consequences for our bad attitudes, something completely under our control.

So how can we stop grumbling and complaining? We can't simply take something away without replacing it. The perfect substitute is gratitude. There is also scientific research regarding gratitude and its effect on our brains and physiology. According to a multitude of studies, gratitude enhances empathy, reduces aggression, brings about better sleep, improves self-esteem, increases mental strength, increases dopamine, lowers anxiety and depression, boosts the immune system, and makes us more productive. Whew! That's a whole lot of benefits!

We tell our kids all the time it's okay to be different—and we absolutely mean it! We know in our hearts that *different* is just what the world needs. Likewise, our Father calls you and me to be different. He says to let our lights shine in the darkness (Matthew 5:16). We live in a dark world that knocks us down and dampens our joy. So, let's make our homes a bright place where our spouse can retreat from the dark and refuel in light—a place where gratitude lives and grows, where good news is shared, and where God's hand of provision is expected and sought.

When Joel repairs the car, a simple sentence expressing my thanks is enough to put wind in his sails. When he thanks me for making a meal and doing the dishes—even though I do this every day—it makes me feel appreciated and valued. Simple gratitude goes a long way.

Discuss It: What current situation has you grumbling? Is there something good in this situation you can turn your focus toward? What emotions are you transmitting to others lately? How can you foster a spirit of gratitude? How can you make your home a respite from the dark?

Pray Over It: God, forgive us when we choose grumbling over gratitude. Help us to let our lights shine in the darkness and to spread positivity everywhere we go, especially in our own home. We want to turn our home in to a place our family *wants* to be—a place of healing, a place to grow, a place of respite from the hard knocks of life. We need your strength to transform our hearts and minds, from grumbles to gratitude. Amen.

JULY

ACTIVE PURSUIT OF PEACE

Let us therefore make every effort to do what leads to peace and to mutual edification.

ROMANS 14:19

At a time when our children needed daycare for a couple days a week, I (Mandy) was searching for in-home daycares to interview. We visited and interviewed a few that didn't make us feel confident about leaving our children. After going to a house smelling of smoke and another that had terrible "disciplinary" measures, I went home and cried. Joel walked in the room and asked what was wrong. When I told him about my frustration, his reply, "Aww, Honey, it will work itself out." (Side note: He has since learned this was the wrong thing to say.) I cried, "No, it won't! You *think* things work themselves out but it's really *me* working them out *for* you." Shortly after, I did find the perfect in-home daycare for our family. In fact, our now-teenage daughter is, to this day, best friends with this former babysitter's daughter and has found in them a second family, even going with them on their family vacations.

Maybe some things, like the kink in your neck, eventually work themselves out. Finding a trustworthy daycare, however, does not. Another thing that does not work itself out is peace within a strained relationship. Simply hoping to stumble upon peace won't have the greatest possible outcome. "Make every effort to do what leads to peace," Paul says. We are to be *actively pursuing* peace. Some translations say to "follow after peace." We are to be peace chasers, to run hard after peace, to fight for peace.

The opposite of fight is flight, or avoidance. Are we running after peace? Or are we passively standing still, hoping peace drops into our laps? When we're at odds with someone, it's excellent to forgive, but we can't just quietly forgive in our hearts and hope the relationship will heal on its own. We are to pursue peace and restore the relationships with the ones we've forgiven. We are to do what it takes, as far as is in our power, to bring that relationship to the point of no tension. Build the bridge and bury the hatchet along with the hostility.

Some think making peace means we must come to an agreement, that we must win others to our point of view or there will be no peace. However, if we believe this, we believe a lie. We can disagree and still have peace. When we're staying home from family functions to avoid a family member with differing political or religious views, we have missed the mark. We have lit dynamite under the bridge to peace. If disagreeing adults can have enough respect for one another to listen to the other—listen for the purpose of learning and loving—civil discussions can be eye-opening and educational. However, if emotions run too deep and opinions are too fiercely expressed, it's a good idea to deem that topic off-limits for the sake of peace. Isn't it better to find a common ground to build your relationship than to avoid the relationship altogether?

In marriage, actively pursuing peace means we aren't waiting for an apology before forgiving, we aren't waiting days to iron out a conflict that turned into a hot mess, and we are seeking to understand our spouse's viewpoint before pressing our own. As one might seek buried treasure, may we spare no effort in fighting for peace in our marriages.

Discuss It: Outside of marriage, what troubled relationships come to mind today? Have you been hoping it would naturally start moving in a positive direction but haven't taken steps in the pursuit of peace? Within your marriage, how quickly do you try to resolve conflict? Do you wait for an apology before forgiving? (If you're ready to take steps toward peace, the next devotion is full of ideas for actively pursuing peace.)

Pray Over It: God of Peace, thank you for the peace you give us, the peace that transcends our own understanding. Although it feels good when others agree with us, we realize making multiple people who think and act just like us is not your plan. We choose peace in all circumstances because you are the God of Peace and you desire peace for our lives, our family, our friendships, and our marriage. Bring healing to our broken relationships. Teach us how to actively pursue peace. Amen.

HOW TO PURSUE PEACE

*Let us therefore make every effort to do what
leads to peace and to mutual edification.*

ROMANS 14:19

As we learned in the previous devotion, we are to *actively pursue* peace in all relationships. This is a big calling. Where do we begin? How do we pursue peace with people we don't agree with?

Part of the pathway to peace is prevention. Doves, the symbols of peace, are like any other bird in that any slight commotion makes them fly away. In similar fashion, we must be careful how we speak and act or we'll cause peace to fly out of sight. If the words on the tip of our tongue could wedge us deeper into discord, we need to make an about-face. This means we're not going to point out to the one taking offense to what we said that they recently said the same thing to us. We're not going close the door on peace by saying things like, "I'm done with you." We're not going to attack another's character or speak in a way that belittles another, like, "If you side with this view, you're an idiot." We won't immediately shoot down others' ideas, even when they're undoubtedly wrong. If we listen with love and respect and make sure others feel heard, they won't feel the need to escalate.

Many of us wish for peace but are not pursuing the things that make peace. We are holding on to peace slayers such as pride and the need to be right. We have not yet learned that peace is far more deeply satisfying than "being right." Obtaining peace requires humility, self-denial, respect, and loving others more than ourselves. Let's set aside our need to "be right" for the sake of harmony. Sometimes admitting we make mistakes or may have been wrong feels like dying because, well, we're killing our pride. But this death leads to life!

Actively pursuing peace means we aren't waiting around for an apology to make amends. Instead, we apologize first, even if we did nothing wrong. Matthew 5:23-24 directs us to initiate reconciliation, even if it is the other person who has the problem with us. Apologizing moves a conversation in the direction of peace, softens hearts, and disarms those whom, moments ago, stood ready to fire. It may even prompt them to examine their own part in the problem. However, sometimes we don't get their apology, and we have to be okay with that. We need to take whatever sliver of peace the other is willing to offer.

When strong emotions are involved, our perception becomes clouded. We see things that were never there. We hear things that were never said. We must accept there is a very strong possibility both ourselves and those who have wronged us have been misunderstood. We need to leave room for being wrong in our perceptions and give grace to those who've misperceived us.

If our offenders are unaware they have offended us and aren't continuing to hurt us, it may be best to forgive in our hearts, let go of our grudges in a low-key way, and move forward without bringing it to our offender's attention. Sometimes, to keep the peace, it is best to let sleeping dogs lie. However, if bitterness has settled in, what may appear as a sleeping dog, might be a cat ready to pounce. If that's the case, pursuing peace through a conversation is best.

At times when confrontation is needed to make peace, it's a good idea to have other non-involved people listen to what we plan to say or read what we have written. Ask how the words and tone might come across. Sometimes our thoughts aren't accurately portrayed in the way we say things and can easily be taken the wrong way. If there's even a shred of animosity, it can be communicated unintentionally. Lastly, it's a good idea to ask ourselves three questions before confronting. *Is it kind? Is it true? Is it necessary?*

At times, we try to reconcile but are put in a no-win situation. Sometimes, others flat-out lie about what they actually did, or didn't, do. Sometimes, they won't confess they lied. Some people can only see from their own perspective, not another's. There will be times we will have no reconciliation and we must forgive without an apology. That may be the only tool available to reach peace. But we must take whatever sliver we can. Relationships are more important that being right.

Sometimes, it's easier not to try to reconcile with others—just brush it under the rug and move on without the person who rubbed us the wrong way. However, that is our human nature, not God's plan for our lives. When we're in the state of mind we don't even desire reconciliation, we need a heart change. To get to the place we *desire* God's plan for reconciliation, we need to pray for others. Not pray they would change, not pray they would apologize, not pray they would pay for what they did, but pray *for* them. Pray good things will come to them. Pray God's blessings over them. Pray to see them as God sees them. Our own hearts are transformed in a powerful, miraculous way when we pray for those who challenge and stretch us, and we earnestly seek the best for them.

The last part of Romans 14:19 says we are to do what leads to edification. The Greek for *edification* is *oikodomēs,* which means to build up. Are we building others up or tearing them down? Are we facilitating healing or are we further wounding? Are we instilling confidence or incapacitating? If we're focused on the positive traits in others and giving them encouragement, we're inviting peace to come and stay a while in our lives.

Choose peace. Chase it down. Hold it tightly.

Discuss It: How can you actively pursue peace in a tense relationship? What could you lay aside for the sake of peace? For what good things could you be praying over others who've wronged you? Do you make peace priority over "being right"? What are the sources of tension in your home? How can you actively pursue peace at home? Consider whether your words to your spouse are tearing them down or building them up. Consider allowing your spouse to "be right" for the sake of peace. Consider how you can be more intentional about instilling confidence in your spouse.

Pray Over It: God of Peace, forgive us for the times we have allowed our pride and arrogance to cause tension in our relationships, both outside the marriage and within the marriage. We lay aside our pride and our need to be right. We pray good things for [name your offender and some good things you hope for them]. Help us to take the right steps toward making amends with them. Soften their heart, and ours as well, so we may establish peace as you wish. Please help us make peace priority in our marriage over any selfish desire we may have. Amen.

SURELY, NOT EVERYTHING, RIGHT?

*In the same way, those of you who do not give up
everything you have cannot be my disciples.*

Luke 14:33

What?! Jesus wants us to give up everything we have? By the time Jesus made this far-reaching statement, he had quite the following. Large crowds had been tagging along with him as he traveled, curious and captivated, but not committed. Jesus wanted to make clear to them, before they decided to follow him, the cost of being his disciple was steep: they would have to give up everything they had.

Disciple means learner. To learn from Jesus means more than merely listening to a sermon. Learning requires action. The action? Sacrifice. Jesus knew there were people in the crowd following him simply because he inspired them. They weren't there for the life change. He gave thought-provoking messages, offered healing for incurable diseases, and granted forgiveness and salvation to those hungry for hope. For many following him then (and for some of us today), it was solely about what he could do for them, about miracles, about attaining blessings for themselves. To be a true follower of Jesus meant something more, something most people didn't (and still don't) bargain for. His way goes deeper, requiring sacrifice and commitment, an extreme and transformational investment.

How extreme an investment? Everything. Every. Single. Thing.

One might think, after reading this verse, Jesus requires us to sell everything we own and leave our families, to follow him. But when we look at the story of Zacchaeus, we see Zacchaeus decided to give half of everything he had to the poor and to pay back four times the amount he had cheated the people. That was enough for Jesus to reach and change Zacchaeus. And, although Levi "left everything and followed him," we are then told Levi "held a great banquet for Jesus at his house" (Luke 5:27-29). Apparently, Levi didn't give up his house but was still considered a follower. In addition, we find many of the disciples who followed Jesus retained some of their possessions. John took Jesus's mother into his home after the crucifixion (John 19:27). A few of the disciples were using their boats and nets to fish when Jesus appeared to them following the resurrection (John 21:1-14).

Clearly, Jesus didn't intend for us to literally get rid of everything we own. So, what did he mean? We can conclude Jesus was speaking about priorities. We are being called to part with anything that gets in our way of serving him. We should be ready, whenever he may call, to sacrifice anything and everything for his sake. We can hold nothing too tightly but come to him with open hands. "Giving up everything" means when God asks it of us, at the drop of a hat, we give without hesitation, unhindered and unconstrained.

God wants top priority in our lives. He is jealous for us when we put anything before him (Exodus 20:5). Whether it be money, material possessions, relationships, or our plans. If anything becomes more important than his place in our lives or hinders our growing relationship with him, then it needs to go.

As always, Jesus directs us to look at our hearts. Are we willing to give *all* if it were asked of us? Or are we holding too tightly to the objects we've acquired in this temporary kingdom? What, when you think of sacrificing it, leaves you unsettled and apprehensive? What would be too difficult for you to give up—your dream home, your car, your hobby, entertainment, comfort, an unhealthy habit, a relationship you've prioritized over him, a relationship dragging you away from him, your position in your career…?

Jesus says it is difficult for "someone who is rich" to enter the Kingdom of Heaven (Matthew 19:24). This may be so because the more we have, the more difficult it is for us when we are asked to let go. Luke 12:48 says for him who is given much, *of him* much will be demanded. Before you go thinking you aren't in the "much will be demanded" group, if you're American, you are rich. The poorest American is richer than eighty percent of the world.

Money is a hot topic for arguments in a marriage. One spouse is the spender while the other is the saver. One wants to put the annual work bonus toward house remodeling while the other wants to use it for vacations. One pushes further into debt while the other becomes increasingly resentful. Finances are a breeding ground for disagreements. We—Joel and Mandy—were opposite in our views regarding spending, saving, and giving. Over the years, as we have learned more about God's plan for our finances, we have grown to agree over our budget—how much we give, what amount we spend, and to what extent we save.

If finances are a touchy subject in your marriage, use Jesus's teaching as a guide to come to an agreement. Pray for a unified direction. If your heart is reluctant to let go of whatever it is God is calling you to surrender, pray God will change your heart to *desire* what he asks of you.

Though we may feel God demands more than we can give, let's remember: He empowers us to do anything and everything he asks of us. We need only be willing, and he will take our hand and walk with us as we walk those steps out in faith.

Discuss It: How do you differ from your spouse when it comes to financial decisions? What are you holding onto a little too tightly? Is there anything you would not be willing to part with? Have you been called to sacrifice something but shrugged it off because it demanded *just too much*? What has Jesus called you to abandon to fully follow him?

Pray Over It: Savior, sometimes you ask us to sacrifice, but we don't want to let go of our things and our comforts. Forgive us for the times we have prioritized comfort over sacrifice and stagnation over growing in our relationship with you. Help us to reprioritize the things we hold dear. May we be on the same page regarding our financial direction and goals. We pray we would hold our things and comforts so loosely that we could toss them aside in an instant with no hesitations. We trust what you have in store for us is worth every sacrifice. Amen.

SIMPLY OVERSEERS

*In the same way, those of you who do not give up
everything you have cannot be my disciples.*

LUKE 14:33

In the previous devotion, we learned Jesus requires us to give up anything that hinders us from learning, from growing in our faith, or from serving Christ. Anything and everything is on the table as a potential sacrifice. We can have things, but we need to rethink our "ownership" of the things we have. When we follow Christ, not only do we belong to him, everything we "own" is his. That make us simply overseers of the things in our possession.

Most of us would love to keep our comfortable lives and slide God somewhere in the cracks where we are lacking. Or we want to spend our money on "stuff" to improve our lifestyle, and then give only whatever is left over. But we can't just add Jesus to our greedy, consumerist lifestyle as a way of taking care of a spiritual need. When we commit our lives to Christ, we really commit everything. The Greek word for *give up* in this verse is *apotassetai,* which means to renounce. As followers of Jesus, we renounce ownership, or surrender the deed, to all we own. We acknowledge that nothing is our own, not even our own spirits or our own bodies (1 Corinthians 6:19-20). He owns it all. We are simply overseers. So, when he asks us to give up something or shift "oversight" of what we "own" to someone else, we must follow his orders.

When our daughter was three years old, she fought with her brother over a balloon she received. I told her everything in this world belongs to God, including the balloon, and that even though God lets us use things, he wants us to share them. Our daughter took the lesson to heart and easily shared the balloon with her brother. Several hours later, when the conversation was off her mind, the balloon in the next room randomly popped. Our daughter gasped in surprise, "That was God's balloon!" I imagine she was bewildered as to why God would want to pop his balloon. May we get to the point where we can say after "our" balloon pops (or our cherished family heirloom breaks, our dream home is lost, our valued material item is loaned to some-one in need, our peaceful environment is sacrificed for a ministry, our free time is spent on less-than-gratifying demands), "That is God's, and he can do with it as he chooses."

What are you holding onto with a tight grasp? What would be difficult for you to give up if God nudged you to do so? Here are a few examples to spark your thoughts:

- Your free time on a Saturday to help someone on bedrest.

- A downsize from the vehicle that has you strapped financially to a car that's not quite the statement you want to make.

- The use of your home for a church or Bible study gathering.

- A move into a smaller house to reduce debt.

- A laughter-filled night out with friends to sit instead with a grieving friend.

- Negative self-talk and pity parties for confidence in God.

- The triumph of winning an argument at the price of anoth-er's dignity.

- A move to a third-world country to help them gain access to clean water and education in agriculture.

- A new 9:00 bedtime to face the next day with a good attitude.

- TV time in exchange for reading devotions with the kids.

- A friend who leads you into temptation.

- Your favorite music that leads your thoughts astray.

If the idea of surrendering any of these suggestions caused a twinge of unease inside you, consider that an area you may be holding too tightly.

Take a mental inventory of every material possession you "oversee" and how you spend your time. Consider what God would have you do with each: your house, car, vacation money, hobbies, "giving" budget, free time, lifestyle... Discuss with your spouse what God wants for every bit. If one of you doesn't have clarity, pray God would reveal his will to you both in an obvious way.

A faith that costs nothing is worth nothing. Before we consider "everything" too much to sacrifice, let's remember the prize we win is worth the price we pay. Jesus promises our sacrifices will be repaid one hundred times (Mark 10:28-31). He wants our focus, not on the here-and-now where our things can be taken, destroyed, and left behind, but on the eternal Kingdom (Matthew 6:19-21). And in Matthew 6:33, he tells us when we focus on him and his Kingdom, we will have not only a reward in the future, but our needs for the here-and-now met.

You may have seen a popular meme with a picture of a little girl holding a teddy bear and Jesus reaching to take it while she says, "But I love it, God..." Jesus is saying, "Just trust me..." What the girl doesn't see is Jesus holding a larger teddy bear behind his back, ready to give in exchange if she would just let go of that small bear.

We can't tell you what he's asking of you—that is for you and your spouse to learn. We have known people who gave up, not just a few cans of soup or a shirt they no longer wear, but large items that required much sacrifice on their part, such as a car or a brand-new washing machine and dryer. We can't know what he's asking of us if we don't tune in to him, learn his heart, learn his ways, and pray for clarification on what he wants of us. We must be willing to let go of the life we thought we wanted for his promise of something better.

Discuss It: Would you consider God to be the Lord over your finances and possessions? What, when you think of it being taken from you, causes anxiety in you? Of the listed ideas for sacrifice, which causes a bit of unease? Have you felt a prompting to give up something, or to use something you "own," for God's glory? How is your life a reflection of what you have given up for God? Do you think others see your pursuit of Jesus as top priority over everything?

Pray Over It: Proprietor of our lives and everything we own, we relinquish the deed to all we have. We realize we are simply overseers of the things you have placed in our care. Please make clear to us your will for the things we oversee. Change our hearts until we view the relationship we have with our things in the light it should be viewed. We pray nothing in our clutch would hinder our growth or your glory. Amen.

AUGUST

OUR OPINIONS & STUBBORNNESS

Fools find no pleasure in understanding but delight in airing their own opinions.

PROVERBS 18:2

Think about the way we humans enter the world, without knowledge of how to use even our own hands, but quickly finding a way to boldly scream to others. Even as we develop into children and teens, we can barely see outside ourselves. Conveniently, our opinions are usually self-serving. Some of us are stuck in that early stage of uninformed and selfish opinions, not aware or simply not caring enough, to look at the big picture before drawing our conclusions. It's not until we mature and develop a sense of those around us that we seek to understand others and allow change in our opinions.

Opinions are often formed without graciousness or consideration. It could be, when you're running late to your meeting, the slow driver in front of you is not being inconsiderate but is just coming back on the road after a bad accident. It could be your unfriendly or forgetful waitress is not incompetent but rather in the process of a bad break up. It could be your wife wants to talk through your whole movie, not because she wants to annoy you, but because she really needs your company and connection. It could be your husband isn't selfish by not helping with the housework, but he doesn't realize just how much time is required to maintain it. It could be your wife has been quiet, not because she is giving you the silent treatment to manipulate you, but she needs time to gather her thoughts before she says something she'll regret.

141

When we withhold our opinions, or accusations, in favor of grace, we often gain a new understanding of the situation, and it shifts our judgement. Understanding is a floodlight that dispels the darkness of judgement. It's best to give the benefit of the doubt to others freely, graciously, and automatically.

Fault-finding opinions are a sure-fire way to start, or prolong, an argument. To avoid accusing your spouse and raising his or her defenses, try this healthy communication technique: Make "I Statements" instead of "You Statements." "You Statements" are accusatory and lead to raised defenses. In contrast, "I Statements" focus on how another's actions made you feel and are much more productive in resolving issues. Instead of saying, "You keep interrupting me," try, "I feel like my thoughts aren't important when I don't get to finish expressing what's in my head." Instead of, "You're always nitpicking everything I do," try, "I feel degraded when I'm not trusted to make even the most minor decisions for myself." Instead of saying, "You never help me around the house," try saying, "I feel overwhelmed by the housework piling up. I really need help."

Opinions can also be damaging when we won't change them after learning they are wrong. That is stubbornness. There are beneficial qualities to stubbornness—the ability to persevere when the odds are against us, not allowing the impossible to deter our efforts, and inspiring others to persevere, come to mind. However, stubbornness has negative qualities as well. Without having the whole picture, we can be fueled with unnecessary anger against those who don't agree with us. We are deterred from asking for help when we really need it. We don't admit we're in the wrong or take responsibility for our own wrong-doings.

In our stubbornness, we often think if another person can change our minds, we are indecisive and cowardly. Having the ability to change our minds after discovering new information does not make us spineless and wishy-washy. It makes us wise. It's okay to say, *I don't know enough about this to form an opinion.* It doesn't make us weak-minded, but instead mature, thoughtful, introspective, and wise. We may think our spouse won't respect us if we don't have all the answers or if we admit we were wrong. But it's quite the opposite. They will regard our opinions highly when they know we are guided by grace and understanding.

Ephesians 4:29 says, "Do not let any unwholesome talk come out of your mouths, but only what is helpful for building others up according to their needs, that it may benefit those who listen." Let's think about how our opinions will affect the people around us. Our opinions may be true, but will they build someone up? If not, let's be wise and keep them to ourselves.

Discuss It: Do others consider you to be an opinionated or stubborn person? Look at the paragraph listing the pros and cons of stubbornness (fifth paragraph). Do you see any of those negative or positive qualities in yourself? Think about the strong opinions you hold. In what situation might you have been uninformed of all the details and wrongly accused someone? Practice with your spouse right now using "I Statements." Take a subject you have recently argued about and turn it into an "I Statement." In what situations can you offer the benefit of the doubt? How can you build others up with your opinions?

Pray Over It: Father, forgive us when we have drawn conclusions based on our limited knowledge. Forgive us for placing so much worth on our opinions that it has wedged its way into our relationships and caused division. Help us to keep our mouths shut when our opinions will not build another up. We pray we would maintain the good qualities of stubbornness and dispose of the negative. Amen.

PLEASURE IN UNDERSTANDING

*Fools find no pleasure in understanding but
delight in airing their own opinions.*

PROVERBS 18:2

We can gather from Proverbs 18:2 that, unless we are fools, we will find pleasure in understanding. When we seek to understand, our desire to gain knowledge and insight is stronger than our desire to air our own opinions. How many of us can honestly say we would rather understand other people than share our own thoughts, opinions, and where we stand on things? It's a lofty goal but this verse suggests we'll find pleasure on our journey there.

Seeking to understand means we strive to gain insight into others' lives, motivations, and viewpoints. Consequently, we give grace when we would otherwise judge. Sometimes we forget how painful it felt to be misunderstood or judged. At one point, we were judged—we wanted to give insight into our lives and dismiss the false accusations. We would do well to remember how that felt—to put ourselves in another's shoes—for then we can offer to others what we had longed for—understanding and grace.

Seeking to understand means we listen more than we talk—listen to learn and gain insight rather than "listen" to form a response. Listen by asking questions of others, not for the purpose of "poking holes" in their argument, but for gaining a new perspective. Even if we ultimately don't agree with the other perspective, there is joy and peace when we attempt to "see" others. There is joy when we give people a piece of our heart rather than a piece of our mind.

145

Seeking to understand means we are open to looking at ourselves as others might perceive us. It's easy to give others the wrong impression. Mandy's face doesn't usually match her heart and thoughts. When she came to understand her face gives off an angry expression when she's deep in thought (even deep in thought about something positive), she could work on lightening her expression and becoming more intentional about smiling.

If it's so easy for others to get the wrong idea about us, consider how easy it is for us to get the wrong impression of others. Again, insight and understanding lead to grace.

Maybe others are wrong. But maybe *we're* wrong. When we're clearly in the wrong, brushing it under the rug doesn't make us look less wrong. It makes us look prideful. There is no pleasure in being corrected and seeing our wrong. Not at first. But there is even less pleasure when others avoid us because we can't look at our wrongdoings and self-improve. What the world desperately needs is for each of us to have a better attitude about correction. When confronted with the idea that our ways, thoughts, and opinions are wrong, instead of instantly putting up our defenses and spewing out excuses, let's make it a habit to initially not respond at all. Take a few days after a confrontation to question it and pray about it. Let's have the courage to ask someone else, a close friend who will tell us the truth in love, before we chuck the idea. With this habit of openness and self-evaluation, may we find others desire, instead of dread, our presence. There is pleasure in that.

Another way to gain understanding, is to surround ourselves with wise people. Ask them questions and observe their interactions with others. Mandy was touring the Florida Everglades with her cousins when they came across a deer standing in a mucky pond up to the top of his legs. He had green plants and pond moss across his back, dripping down his sides. The tour guide told them he had been abandoned as a baby and was raised by the water buffalo. He became a part of their herd and he thought he was a water buffalo! In the same way, we become like those with whom we surround ourselves. If we hang with those who air their opinions without interest in gaining insight into others' viewpoints, we are limiting ourselves to mucky ponds. If we are intentional about spending time with those who seek to learn from others, to love and accept others, and to gain insight into their lives, their approach to life—seeking insight—will rub off on us. We will hop and run freely as deer.

For us married people, how many times have we jumped to the wrong conclusion about our spouse without attempting to gain insight and understanding? How many arguments could we have spared ourselves by asking questions, listening, and walking in his or her shoes for a moment before accusing? Before we jump to conclusions, let's attempt to understand each other—pause before we pounce.

Listen. Learn. Gain insight. Self-evaluate. Remain open to correction. Walk in another's shoes. Open your heart to understand another. These are the things that will bring pleasure.

Discuss It: Would you say you attempt to truly understand others? In what ways could you attempt to gain understanding in your marriage? Would you say you are open to self-evaluation and correction? Can you think of a recent time you gave someone a piece of your mind? How could you, instead, have given them a piece of your heart? Who in your life do you consider wiser than yourself? How can you be intentional about spending more time with him or her?

Pray Over It: Dear God, we know you did not promise us a life without difficulty. Instead, you promised to freely give wisdom to any who ask for it. God, we are asking for that wisdom. Please remind us not to jump to conclusions, but to gain understanding. Being criticized makes us feel uncomfortable. However, we pray you will give us the ability to receive criticism constructively. We pray we would not allow criticism to defeat us, but to change us. Help us to find pleasure in understanding. Amen.

WAITING FOR LOVE

Love is patient, love is kind. It does not
envy, it does not boast, it is not proud.

1 Corinthians 13:4

We're all in love with the idea of love, but the sacrifices we must make to maintain love in our personal lives prove to be challenging. Things like holding our tongue, surrendering our will, parting with something we enjoy, and letting go of offenses are a few. Sometimes these sacrifices are required to keep something that matters more: relationships.

There are four words to describe *love* in the Greek language. A brotherly/friendship love, *philia;* a romantic love, *eros;* a familial love, *storge*; and *agape.* In this verse, the word *agape* is used. Agape is a self-sacrificing love given without demands, expectations of repayment, or ulterior motives. It is not given out of pride, for a pat on the back, or for personal gain, and no condition must be met by the receiver. Agape love has little to do with the feeling of love and much to do with self-denial for the sake of another, with another's best interest in mind. Agape love offers acts of service given not only to the easy-to-love but to the obnoxious, intolerable, unlovable *and* that one difficult family member. The second greatest commandment (after the first which is to love God with everything in us) is to love others, *all* of them.

Agape love is awakened when we realize God's agape love for us. We only understand agape love because he agape-loved us first (1 John 4:19). We will never be able to truly agape-love someone until we have first grasped how wide, long, high, and deep is his love and sacrifice for us (Ephesians 3:18). When we experience God's love and comprehend our worth, we have so much more agape love to give, not from our broken, empty heart which has been hurt by the world but from a heart completely repaired and filled to its rim by him.

Paul further details how agape love is expressed. He doesn't simply give us this lofty goal of agape love and say, "Off you go! Good luck!" His teaching moves farther, right into the daily grind of our everyday lives.

He tells us love is patient. This is not the kind of patience we use when we're in a hurry and stuck in traffic. The Greek word for *patience* used here is a long-tempered type of patience. It is slow to anger, endures offenses without retaliation, gives grace to others when they make mistakes, and respects people who have different views. This type of patience attempts to understand others through compassion rather than keeps them at a distance because we can't relate. It desires for others to reach their potential. It patiently waits for maturity without criticism.

Throughout history, God himself displays this long-suffering type of patience. The book of Hosea portrays God's patience perfectly. To summarize the story, Hosea was told by God to marry a prostitute, Gomer. Hosea did so, redeeming her from her painful existence, and bringing her into his unmerited love. They were happy and had a son together. But it was not long before Gomer became ungrateful and restless. She broke Hosea's heart as she left him time and time again, chasing other lovers and even bearing children in his house that were not his. God told Hosea to continue taking her back. Then the final blow. Gomer left him again, only this time, she fell into the hands of slave traders. This dreadful day, Gomer was up for sale as a slave. Hosea, under God's instruction, did the unthinkable. Despite his own pain and the shame brought on him by her disloyalty, he bought her from the slave block to make her his wife once again.

This beautiful allegory demonstrates God's loving patience for his people. Hosea represents God, while Gomer represents God's people. Despite our constant rejection of him, God continues to pursue us and buy us back with his ultimate sacrifice for us.

This is the kind of patience God has called us to, not simple tolerance. When God asks us to forgive, to offer grace, and to wait patiently for others to grow, he's not asking us to do something he, himself, hasn't done for us time and time again.

(Side note: God isn't saying you *must* take back your spouse who has had an affair (Matthew 19:9). He is demonstrating the depth of his own long-suffering patience with us. If your spouse has been unfaithful, we urge you to pray and seek outside Christian counsel for direction.)

God extends to us infinite, long-tempered patience and requires us to extend this long-tempered patience to one another. We may feel our spouse is not growing, maturing, and gaining wisdom as quickly as *we* did or to their fullest potential. Nonetheless, we should wait patiently, without pressuring, and without criticism. When we're patient, we are slow to anger and quick to forgive. When the first thought jumping into our heads is, *you're an idiot*, long-tempered patience chooses to give the benefit of the doubt and still show them respect. Patience attempts to understand another with compassion and releases control when another chooses differently.

Maybe due to past hurts, out of self-protection, you've closed part of your heart to your spouse. Maybe your spouse is continuing to hurt you and there are necessary boundaries in place. But *maybe*, your spouse has been improving, working to gain back your trust, has not hurt you in a long time, yet, you still haven't re-opened that part of your heart. Maybe it's time to open it again. Pray about it and listen for God's direction.

When an abusive family member is radically changed by Jesus, it is common for the other members of the family to feel, not so much gratitude, but resentment that it took so long—so much pain they endured as they waited for the change. It's normal for it to feel not fair. But fair isn't how God works. If God were all about fairness, then he wouldn't have sent Jesus to take our punishment. God is all about grace, long-suffering patience, and forgiveness.

If we're going to accept God's long-tempered patience for us, then we must be willing to give it to others, especially our spouse.

Discuss It: Is there a person in your life who requires this long-tempered type of patience from you? How would your relationships—with family or friends, at work, in church—look different if you were expressing love with this long-tempered type of patience? In what way do you often lose patience with your spouse? Answer these introspectively: Has your heart closed to your spouse due to past hurts? Could you consider re-opening your heart? How could you make a better attempt to understand your spouse with loving compassion? In what way do you need to improve in the department of long-tempered patience?

Pray Over It: God, your patience with us is astounding! We know we've let you down and broken your heart, yet you keep taking us back time after time. Please give us strength to offer second chances (and third and fourth…) and to remain open-hearted to those who have hurt us, especially to one another. We can't do it on our own. We need your help. May we offer grace always and give one another the benefit of the doubt. Amen.

PRACTICAL BENDING

Love is patient, love is kind. It does not
envy, it does not boast, it is not proud.

1 Corinthians 13:4

What costs nothing but means everything? Kindness. Paul teaches *agape* love is kind. The Greek word for *kind* Paul used here comes from a word meaning both useful and gentle. So, in essence, kindness searches for opportunities to be useful to others in gentle and practical ways. It bends to become what others need it to be.

There are many ways to show kindness: encouraging comments, whether through a verbal compliment, a handwritten letter, or affirmational text; listening ears; a shoulder to cry on; a conversation with a stranger who is obviously longing for someone to talk with; a thoughtful gift; a positive comment to brighten someone's day; an allowance for the hurried shopper to cut in line; a party invitation to someone not currently in our friend-circle; or a meal for someone under stress.

Opportunities to show kindness are infinite. We will see the needs all around us if we just open our eyes and pay attention to others—whether strangers, friends, or family—we will see the needs in every place we go. Sometimes we see a need but feel at a loss for how to meet the need. We can pray for wisdom in meeting that need, ask others who have been in similar situations what they would have wanted during that time, or research ideas in meeting that need. Sometimes we are surprised, but the smallest gestures can make a world of difference!

We have been on the receiving end of kindness countless times. Sometimes it was the thing that kept us going when we wanted to throw in the towel. When we were buried in the throes of a difficult parenting situation, a card from a friend came in the mail with words of encouragement that were like balm to our weary souls. When Mandy was diagnosed with cancer, some friends put together a fund-raiser to help us with the unexpected costs. A mentor came alongside me (Joel), allowed me to vent, and prayed with me. When going through family difficulties, Mandy's friend bombarded her with encouraging and funny texts. Kindness comes in all forms, whatever form it needs to bend into, and is a valuable medicine for a hurting world.

Even if we go out of our way to show kindness to others, all too often, we let our spouse fall by the wayside. Many times, we slide into a way of life as if our spouse is a roommate rather than a lover. We're simply tag-teaming with taking care of the kids and facing the daily grind on autopilot. Romance forgotten. It's easy to get lost in our daily routines and responsibilities and forget how much it means to our spouse for us to step outside our normal routine and do something extra, something kind.

Kindness is a great way to move our marriage out of the rut and keep the spark alive. Here are a few practical ideas: give her a few hours on a Saturday to do whatever she wants, drop off a romantic note to his work, ask how you can help her clean, clean his car for him, pick up her favorite treat on your way home from work, text him in the middle of the day a few reasons you love him. These quick, easy gestures show you care and will mean more to your spouse than you would imagine! I still remember when Mandy brought a home-made pie to my work for no reason other than to brighten my day. It made all my coworkers jealous, and I still remember it twenty years later. A small act of kindness can make ripples for years.

Marriage In Abundance provides married couples with marriage challenges — ideas to serve one another, to encourage each other, and to rekindle the romance. It's easy to get caught up in the responsibilities of life and forget to bring intentional kindness into the marriage. The marriage challenges remind you, right in the middle of your daily grind, to bring that act of kindness or to slip in some intimacy — to keep you out of "roommate" status with your spouse. If you're not already participating in Marriage In Abundance's marriage challenges, check out how at www.marriaginabundance.com.

Discuss It: Recall a time someone outside your home extended kindness to you in just the right moment of need. In what practical ways could you show kindness in the workplace? In your extended family? With your kids? With friends? With a stranger? Think of a way to step outside your normal responsibilities and show kindness to your spouse this week. Plan it right now.

Pray Over It: Kind Father, sometimes we're oblivious to the needs around us. Open our eyes to the opportunities surrounding us every day. Help us to not be so self-absorbed we miss chances to demonstrate your love to others. When we see others in need, please show us ways to relieve their burdens, give them hope, and keep them moving forward by blowing a little wind in their sails. Give us practical ideas to show kindness to one another. Please open a time slot in our busy schedules to make our marriage priority. May we show kindness to one another and keep our marriage spark alive. Amen.

SEPTEMBER

THOUGHTS TO REALITY

*Finally, brothers and sisters, whatever is true, whatever
is noble, whatever is right, whatever is pure, whatever
is lovely, whatever is admirable—if anything is
excellent or praiseworthy—think about such things.*

PHILIPPIANS 4:8

Changing our quality of life is possible through changing our thoughts. This doesn't seem feasible, but it's scientifically proven. The *Law of Concentration* states whatever you consciously and persistently direct your thoughts upon will grow and expand into reality in your life. In other words, the more you think and reflect on something, the larger impact it will have on your daily choices, behavior, and actions. When we constantly dwell on negative thoughts, then negative conditions will increase in our lives. If we dwell on positive thoughts, then pleasant conditions will grow and increase in our lives. What we think about is what we look for, and we usually find what we're looking for.

The Bible addresses this concept in Proverbs 4:23. The NIV says, "Above all else, guard your heart, for everything you do flows from it." The Hebrew word for the *heart* that we are to guard is *leb,* which refers to the will of the inner man. *Leb* could also be translated to mean attention. The New Century Version translates this verse as, "Be careful what you think, because your thoughts run your life."

In some circumstances, we have choices to make. However, sometimes life drops us into situations with zero options. We didn't have a choice about which country or family we were born into. We couldn't choose the way were raised. We can't change the past. We have no control over the weather or the actions of others. Many things in life are beyond our realm of influence. However, we do have control over one thing and that is our thoughts which have more to do with our quality of life than we would imagine.

When we find ourselves up the creek without a paddle, our choices may be limited, but we can still choose our thoughts and beliefs. We can simply endure the difficulty, grit our teeth and bear it—or worse yet, wallow in it—or we can choose to look for, and enjoy, the good in the midst of it. We can grumble about our lemons or squeeze them into water, add some sugar and make the best we can out of them. We can see everything as a tragedy, or we can look for the way God reveals himself in the adversity. We can wallow in self-pity or rise to the challenge as a warrior ready to conquer the enemy. We can focus on the obstacles blocking our way or seek out new opportunities to challenge us and cause us to grow. We can focus on our inadequacy or God's great sufficiency. Choosing to search for the good in life will benefit ourselves, those around us, and our marriages.

Though there are parts of our marriage we can't change, such as our past mistakes or our spouse's character, there are some parts we can, such as the lens in which we view our spouse. That determines the way we treat him or her. If we're ready to change the trajectory of our marriage, it begins with our thoughts.

It's easy to let our frustrations over our spouse pile up until they are all we see. It's also easy to forget why we married our spouse. At some point, our spouse stopped putting his or her best foot forward and so did we, to be honest. Life's challenges swallowed up our fun spirit. Irritations mounted until we now no longer remember what it was that attracted us to our husband or wife—or we remember, but those qualities have been long gone.

Those who run track are trained to keep their eyes focused on where they're going to clear their mind of distractions. In marriage, when we focus on where we want our marriage to be, we will run harder in that direction, clear our heads of distractions, and keep making strides toward that goal of where we want to be. With our focus on the goal, we will have clarity on the minor decisions and make the sacrifices needed to get where we want to be.

It is possible to fall in love with that same person again. It takes mind renewal, a change in our focus. It takes looking for the good in our spouse and letting that be our focus. When a thought pops into mind reflecting any negativity about our spouse, we need to squelch it right away and replace it with something we love about them instead—something true, noble, right, pure, lovely, admirable, excellent, or praiseworthy. Remember, what we look for is what we find. Looking for our spouse's excellent qualities is a powerful gamechanger for our marriages. And it all begins in our thoughts.

Discuss It: Do you tend to see situations with pessimism or optimism? Can you think of a situation that changed once you were able to see it in a new light? What difficult situation are you currently facing? How could you change the way you perceive it? Consider how your thoughts about your spouse are affecting the way you treat him or her and your marriage overall. Write down each of the qualities in this verse—true, noble, right, pure, lovely, admirable, excellent, praiseworthy—and then write a way in which your spouse has demonstrated each quality. Let your thoughts go back to these notes when your attitude needs an adjustment.

Pray Over It: Lord, God, we admit sometimes we feed the negativity in our minds and let it grow. Sometimes we're not even looking for your hand in our hard situations. We pray you would bring awareness to our thoughts. Help us to knead in some fun wherever we can. Change our perspective on life and each other. Point out to us the good qualities in each other and let that be our focus. Amen.

UNITY OF MIND

Finally, all of you, have unity of mind, sympathy,
brotherly love, a tender heart, and a humble mind.

1 PETER 3:8 ESV

When a Christian bad-mouths, snubs, or argues against a fellow Christian, what does that say about Christianity? What does our dissension say about the one whom we serve? Paul suggests we act unified, sympathetic, tender hearted, and humble. Those qualities paint a better picture — a clearer representation of our beautiful God.

First, let's apply this concept to our relationships outside marriage. How can we have "unity of mind" with all our fellow brothers and sisters in Christ when we're all created with different strengths, different qualities, and different personalities? Some of us were given strong wills, while some find surrender easy. Some of us are driven by high ambitions, while some are content and easy-going. Some of us are born leaders, while some are drawn to another's cause. Although, God made us all so different from one another, he still requires unity of mind among us. This doesn't mean we have identical thoughts and ways of doing things. Rather, it is like we are part of an orchestra, all playing to the beat of the same drum. Though we all play different instruments, different notes, even at different times and volumes, we are unified in our goal and purpose, creating one beautiful, harmonious song.

Unity is important to God. "How good and pleasant it is when God's people live together in unity!" we read in Psalm 133:1. Paul recognized the value of unity as well, writing in another letter, "Make every effort to keep the unity of the Spirit through the bond of peace" (Ephesians 4:3). Unity should be important to us as well. But how do we keep the unity when we all have different ideas and views, even different perceptions of the same Scriptures?

Paul spells it out clearly: "Be completely humble and gentle; be patient, bearing with one another in love" (Ephesians 4:2). The New Living Translation puts it this way "…making allowance for each other's faults because of your love." We cover others in the grace we ourselves have been covered. Our attitude should be, *I, too, make mistakes. I love you even still.*

Next, let's apply this to marriage. Marriage is a reflection of our union with Christ (Isaiah 54:5, Ephesians 5:25-27, Revelation 19:7, Revelation 21:2). What kind of image are we portraying when we disrespect our spouse, bicker, and argue with one another? How do we march to the beat of the same drum while playing different instruments? We don't expect our cello of a husband to carry the tune and we don't count on our flute of a wife to fill in with the bass. We support one another's giftings without compromising each other's individual qualities or suppressing the part he or she plays. Sometimes, our instrument rests, allowing the other to shine in solo. Playing background in humility may be required on occasion. At other times, we supplement where the other lacks ability. Sometimes, depending on the circumstance, we even pick up a different instrument. But ultimately, we are playing the same song.

Playing together in harmony takes listening and readjusting. It requires sacrificing our desires for the harmony of the song. It always requires respect. As Paul states, it takes humility, gentleness, patience, and bearing with one another in love. When we are not unified as husband and wife, let's ask ourselves, *Am I being humble? Gentle? Patient? Am I bearing with my spouse in love?* If the answer is *no*, we readjust until our marriage song flows in beautiful harmony.

Discuss It: Think about your church and relationships with other believers. Have you witnessed non-believers repulsed by Christianity due to dissension among Christians? What could have been said or done differently by the Christians for the sake of unity? Consider your marriage. How does your song sound to others — your children, your extended family, and friends? Despite differences, are you playing the same song? In what area is your song cacophonous? How could you play in better harmony? What sacrifices need made, on your part, for a beautiful song?

Pray Over It: Thank you, God, for your Spirit in each of us. We pray you would teach us to have unity within our church and among other believers. May we be indivisible, though we have different ideas on how to complete your missions. Unify us in the decisions we make, the outreach we do, programs we put together, and the way we interact with one another. We pray you would help us, as a couple, to listen, to readjust, and to make the sacrifices we need to make for our marriage to create a harmonious song which brings you glory. Amen.

SYMPATHY, BROTHERLY LOVE, TENDER HEART

Finally, all of you, have unity of mind, sympathy, brotherly love, a tender heart, and a humble mind.

1 PETER 3:8 ESV

What does compassion feel like? It's the feeling we get when we see someone struggling in a difficult situation—physically, mentally, or emotionally—which causes in us a desire to do something to ease their suffering. Sometimes we feel the emotions of others even when we're not in their situation.

Brotherly love comes from the Greek word *philadelphoi, sympathy* from the Greek word, *sympathies,* and *tender heart* from *eusplanchnoi.* All three words point to unity of minds accomplished through compassion, sympathizing, and brotherly love. Compassion means to suffer together, as such, it brings unity by an odd means—through suffering.

It is clear God wants us to have sympathy for one another. He wants us to rejoice with those who rejoice and mourn with those who mourn (Romans 12:15). The opposite—to feel callous, cold, and aloof—is not Christ-like. Even *Jesus wept,* demonstrating his compassion for Mary who was grieving the loss of her brother, Lazarus. John 11:33 tells us, "He was deeply moved in spirit and troubled." If we are to be like him, then we will be moved by others' sorrow and joy. We must first have awareness of the pain of others, then allow our hearts to be moved, and finally, act on that compassion. Jesus simply "feeling" something for Mary wasn't the entirety of Jesus's sympathy. The compassion Jesus expressed was a compassion that drove him to act. When his emotions shifted, he did something about it. He raised this heart-broken woman's brother from the dead.

Compassion without action leaves us feeling empty. So, let's follow Jesus's example — take that compassion we feel for another, allow it to move us in spirit, and then move us to action.

The family of Christians is a support system. We are called to live as a community that comforts, supports, and encourages during the hard times, and celebrates others' victories. We have enough suffering all around us. We are all wounded. The community of Christ should not be where further wounds are created, but instead healed.

Compassion is an essential part of a marriage bond. Some of us were born short-on-compassion and need ideas and practical tips to express compassion to our spouse, so here are a few:

- **Refrain from expressing irritation or cynicism when your spouse is hurting.** Maybe you feel your spouse's emotions are blown out of proportion to the circumstance. If this is the case, don't allow your annoyance to show.

- **Validate your spouse's feelings.** Even if you don't personally share the same feelings about similar situations, shrugging off your spouse's feelings or shaming your spouse for being "overly emotional" doesn't make your spouse feel less emotional. It only puts distance between you.

- **Don't tell them they are acting irrational or blowing things out of proportion due to PMS or being "hangry."** Maybe it's true, but acknowledging their feelings, which are real to them, will go far in keeping you connected.

- **Practice mirroring.** Rather than distancing yourself from the emotions of your spouse that you don't want to feel, try to match their emotions instead. Help them know you are attempting to understand their feelings. For example, if she tells you about a hurtful text from a friend, say, "That is upsetting. I'm sorry you are hurting." Or if he is elated because his overly critical boss finally acknowledged his hard work, put your frustrating day on the back burner and express excitement with him.

- **Show physical affection—a hug, a back rub, a pat on the leg, a brush of fingers through their hair.** Don't underestimate the power of touch.

- **Make a sacrifice to ease their burden.**

- **Greet them pleasantly when they walk in the door; make them feel like their presence matters.**

- **Stay tuned in to their emotional tank.** When it seems to be on empty, shower them with encouragement.

- **Lighten their mood.** Sometimes compassion means cheering their mood with playful comedy, having fun, and laughing together. But humor at the wrong time gives off the impression you don't care. If you want to make them laugh, make sure you are feeling their pain with them before jumping in with humor.

Compassion is the heart of a strong marital bond. Just as a body without a heart won't survive, neither will a healthy marriage without compassion.

Discuss It: Have you experienced the tender-heartedness of a friend or family member in a time of need? When was the last time you were "deeply moved in spirit and troubled" over another's pain? Outside your marriage, in what practical way can you put your compassion into action? Tell your spouse of a time his or her compassion meant a lot to you. In what way can you improve in expressing compassion to your spouse?

Pray Over It: Father, sometimes we get so caught up in our own lives, we forget to look around for the needs of others. Please, help us to notice the pain around us. Move our spirit by others' joy and pain. May we celebrate their victories with them and act to alleviate their sorrow. Give us wisdom and creativity when we feel "moved and troubled in spirit" but are unsure what to do. Help us to remember we, as a married couple, are a team, brought together to support one another in life. May we not distance ourselves emotionally from each other but support one another through compassion. May the compassion in our marriage divide our pain and double our joy. Amen.

THE HUMBLE MIND

*Finally, all of you, have unity of mind, sympathy,
brotherly love, a tender heart, and a humble mind.*

1 PETER 3:8 ESV

Kanye West, a man once full of pride, has said, "I am the number one most impactful artist of our generation."[5] Moreover, he said his greatest pain in life was that he would never be able to see himself perform live. Kanye was a man full of himself. However, after giving his life to Christ, he began to portray a very different man. In his song, "Hands On," he sings that he deserves criticism and has been changed to a man who praises God. He goes from believing he's the best to begging for prayer, laying down his pride, and identifying himself as a man who knows he's in need of grace. The humility is admirable.

Humility means we are willing to take a "lower place" when given the opportunity for a higher position. Humility usually gets a bad rap. It sometimes gets associated with weakness, shame, timidity, and incapability. However, humility is a sign of great strength! When we earn first place, yet choose to allow others to have it, or when the spotlight is on us and we use it to raise up another, it displays incredible strength of mind and will.

Do we admire those who are pushy and self-assertive, desiring power and position over others? Or do we naturally respect those who choose modesty in spirit? People in all cultures tend to establish a "pecking order." Ironically, when we pridefully push ourselves to the top of the pecking order, we are sorely disappointed as others' respect for us drops.

Take this twenty-question "humility test" to determine if you're a humble person or if you could stand to knock your pride down a few notches:

- I can easily acknowledge I don't have it all together.

- I'm okay if others get the credit that belongs to me.

- I put effort into building up others.

- I don't feel a need to defend myself because others' opinions don't define my worth.

- I don't feel a need to tell others about my accomplishments.

- I can continue driving peacefully when a "backseat driver" is telling me to slow down or to take a different route.

- I don't want others to view me as a victim.

- I'm completely open to correction.

- Instead of giving others a "piece of my mind," I can easily say, *Maybe I don't have all the answers, but here are my thoughts for whatever they're worth.*

- I love to cheer others on even when they're ahead of me.

- People who live their lives differently than me don't annoy me. I can easily continue interactions with them.

- I live below my means, in moderation.

- I allow others to choose the restaurants, movies, plans for business actions, and other details.

- I don't look down on others based on the contents in their grocery cart, the clothes they wear, their body shape, their careers, their political views, or their life choices.

- It's okay if I'm seen in public not looking my best.

- I ask others if they want my opinion before offering it to them.

- I am content to listen to another's story without feeling an urge to one-up them with a story of my own.

- When I'm given an important position, I realize it's not because I'm better than others.

- I cannot say there is one person I have not forgiven.

- I realize I still have a lot to learn.

How did we do on the humility test? I'm guessing most of us, myself included, realized we're not as humble as we thought we were. And if we did pass the humility test with flying colors, we may want to check again!

Humility leads us back to unity of mind because we "play well with others." Humility allows sympathy, brotherly love, and a tender heart to guide our lives into unity in community.

Now, let's check our humility level when it comes to marriage with this ten-question quiz:

- I can easily tell my spouse when I realize I've been wrong.

- If my spouse thinks I'm wrong, but I know I'm right, I can drop it and allow them to think I'm wrong.

- When my spouse is hurting, I sympathize with him or her without telling them about a time I had it so much worse.

- When my spouse tells me I hurt him or her, I don't immediately defend myself, but consider how I can resolve it.

- I don't say *I told you so.*

- I don't feel a need to make my spouse do things my way. I allow them to do things their way.

- I ask my spouse for his or her opinion when I'm making decisions.

- I don't believe my spouse is an idiot just because he or she has a different viewpoint than mine.

- I don't believe I am better than my spouse.

- I ask my spouse how I can better meet his or her needs.

Ouch. Pride is the hardest thing to bring down. But once we do, we experience a deeper level of connection with each other. So, let's bring down our pride and allow humility to lift us instead.

Discuss It: What is the hardest part for you in the general humility test? How can you bring that level of pride down? What is the hardest part for you in the marriage humility test? What is God pointing out to you and how will you respond?

Pray Over It: God, we realize we are not as humble as we originally thought. Please take away any desire within us to prove ourselves to others, to look down on others, and [list other areas you struggle with]. Help us to find our confidence and contentment with who we are in you. Help us to see others through the light of your love. We pray we would each bring humility into our marriage and may it deepen our bond with one another. Amen.

OCTOBER

NO RETALIATION

*Don't repay evil for evil. Don't retaliate with insults when people
insult you. Instead, pay them back with a blessing. That is what
God has called you to do, and he will grant you his blessing.*

1 Peter 3:9 nlt

My neighbor was having an in-ground swimming pool built in his
backyard. Another neighbor, irritated by the loud noise of the
construction vehicles during the day, decided to run his lawn mower
at 10:00 p.m. up and down the sidewalk of pool-building neighbor
to "retaliate" for the noise. This is a ridiculous example of retaliation.
However, there are countless hard-core, even disturbing accounts of
vengeance. You, for sure, know of some horrific examples yourself.
Vengeance never goes well, not for the victim nor for the one seeking revenge, and never brings about positive change. Nothing good
comes from revenge—ever.

Revenge isn't found just among neighbors. It has found its way
into our homes. *You yell at me; I'll yell back at you. You buy something
selfishly; I'll treat you like a child. You won't fix the broken doorknob,
then I won't do your laundry. You won't help me around the house, then
I won't sleep with you. You won't do things my way, then I'll give your
family all the dirt on you.* We cannot live like this! Our marriages will
not survive.

When someone wrongs us, it is not within our nature to "let it
go." Naturally, we want them to pay. So, giving in to what feels natural, we step down into the muck to enter their game and the downward spiral begins. We think revenge will relieve our anger; however,
that's not the way it works. Building our happiness on someone else's
unhappiness is backward. Revenge doesn't bring us the happiness or

freedom we thought, in our moment of anger, that it would. The only way to arrive at genuine peace and happiness is to break the cycle of revenge and forgive.

Acknowledging our pain, for a moment, can be beneficial, but then we must leave it behind through prayer. If we decide, instead, to feed the serpent of anger and indignation, it grows, coiling around us until it has choked the life out of us. Dwelling in pain and resentment—allowing another's sin to influence the way *we* live—is destructive to our own selves. We must put an end to animosity for it has the power to destroy everything.

Discuss It: When have you taken revenge on another? How did it end? When did you choose to let go of an offense? How did that end? Consider how you may have treated your spouse poorly, or withheld something good, based on the way he or she treated you. Pray about dropping the charges and letting it go.

Pray Over It: Thank you, Father, for forgiving us, over and over. Reveal to us any grudges we are holding. Please help us to let them go. We need your supernatural power to do this as we're unable in our own strength. Help us to remember, even though it feels unnatural, that it is the best choice for our lives. Amen.

PAYBACK
WITH A BLESSING

Don't repay evil for evil. Don't retaliate with insults when people insult you. Instead, pay them back with a blessing. That is what God has called you to do, and he will grant you his blessing.

1 Peter 3:9 nlt

The Bible not only commands us to forgive those who have wronged us, it goes even further and commands us to pay them back with a blessing! Really?! Someone hurts us and we are to think of a way we can *bless* them?

In the Old Testament, we find many prayers—specifically from David—asking God to destroy his enemies. However, when David was presented with an opportunity, and even urged by his own men, to kill his enemy, David instead spared King Saul's life. David had been running from Saul, living an uncomfortable, nomadic life, hiding in caves, fearing Saul's sword, for years—not days, not months—*years*! Yet, he passed the opportunity to retaliate (1 Samuel 24).

During David's life, the law was "an eye for an eye," paying back aggressions in the same proportion to the offense (Exodus 21:24). Jesus came and turned the law upside-down with grace. Jesus's radical teaching was to love our enemies, pray for them, and even bless them.

Blessing in the Greek is *eulogountes,* which conveys speaking well of another. So, this verse tells us we are to speak well of our enemies. Instead of going around telling everyone the ways we've been wronged, we are to protect the reputation of those who have hurt us.

It's not in our nature, or even in our human power, to wish our enemies well. We need the supernatural power of God to *agape** love those who have wronged us. It's the high road. Anyone can love someone who loves them back, but only with the Spirit can we show love to our enemies and give them what they don't deserve—kindness. To give them what we ourselves have received from God—grace.

Paying back heartache with a blessing sounds ludicrous to us, but God sees the big picture and knows how to break the cycle. Although, pursuing peace by blessing those who have wronged us is not in our nature, it's in his who is within us, and it is the only way to freedom.

Many commands in the Bible, including this command, are followed by a blessing. We are promised in 1 Peter 3:9, when we choose to pay someone back with a blessing instead of retaliation, we will inherit God's blessing. When we respond to others with gentleness and don't allow anxiety to rule our hearts, we are given peace beyond understanding. Peace that doesn't make sense in our circumstances (Philippians 4:5-7). He promises we will be restored after going through bitter troubles (Psalm 71:20). He gives healing where our hearts have been broken (Psalm 147:3). But that healing cannot reach us until the serpent of resentment dies.

In the prior devotion were examples of reasons we might retaliate against our spouse. Maybe he yelled or has been neglecting household chores. Maybe she nitpicked or went way above budget on a pair of shoes. Naturally, we pay back with a nasty comment or by withholding good. But we are to forgive and bless our spouse instead. If the purpose of marriage is to spur each other toward holiness, it is through blessings and constructive words we will help them move toward this goal. Although it's hard—really hard—we are promised God will bless us in return.

Discuss It: Regarding relationships outside your marriage, in what way have you been wronged? In what ways can you bless your transgressor?

---

* *agape*: There are four words used for *love* in the New Testament. *Agape* love is a self-sacrificing love that gives without demands or expectations of repayment, not out of pride or for a pat on the back, has little to do with the feeling of love and much to do with self-denial for the sake of another's best interest. *Agape* is awakened when we realize God's love for us.

Introspection only: What hurt from your spouse has been fresh on your mind? How would you be treating him or her differently if you decided to not withhold any good from your spouse? In what ways can you bless your spouse?

Pray Over It: Father, thank you for blessing us when we didn't deserve it and for teaching us the way to abundant life. We pray you will bless [insert your enemy's name]. God, we know many times people hurt others from a deep pain within themselves. We pray when others lash out at us, we wouldn't take it to heart but put our confidence in your love for us. Please heal [enemy's name]—heal their broken spirit so they may be able to experience meaningful relationships. Give them peace and joy. Give us ideas for ways we can bless them. Give us the energy to climb over the mountain of our hurt and show kindness. Help us to give grace to one another. Give us strength to bless each other when we have been hurt and desire to get back at each other. We pray you would strengthen our marriage through our sacrifice. Amen.

EAGER TO LISTEN

My dear brothers, take note of this: Everyone should be
quick to listen, slow to speak and slow to become angry.

JAMES 1:19

Due to living in this fast-paced culture with modern technology, we are used to getting what we want instantly. We don't like to wait. Forcing ourselves to slow down, to quiet our minds, and to be present in the moment requires effort. And effort is exactly what is required of us to listen when someone is speaking. Listening is a skill and, just as in any other skill, we must put in the effort to cultivate it.

This Scripture says to be "quick to listen." The word *quick* conveys a spirit of eagerness, readiness, and willingness. Remember when we were in school and the boring teacher sounded like the teacher on Charlie Brown, "Wa wap wa wap wa..."? Then, we heard her say, "This will be on the test." Suddenly we tuned in, eager to hear what we needed to know! This is the kind of eagerness we should have when others, including our spouse, are speaking to us.

All too often when others are speaking, we are not really listening. Rather, we are planning what we will say next. Then we interrupt to interject our thoughts before the conversation shifts. Without realizing, we are viewing our thoughts as more important than another's. Philippians 2:3 calls us to view others as more important than ourselves. One way we can do this is through intentional listening, without interjecting our own thoughts. This means we are storing away what we have to say for the moment and absorbing what the other person is telling us. When we view others as more important than ourselves, it follows that we will have genuine interest in what they say.

Listening requires not just putting a plug in your mouth, but intentionally hearing what the other is saying. It is not thinking about the next thing you're going to say, or about the frozen meat you forgot to pull out of the freezer to thaw, or the fact that you once again forgot to call your child's doctor. Intentional listening is a mindful practice—pushing everything out of the mind to deliberately focus on others. Owning three businesses and raising four kids, we can certainly empathize! Having a busy lifestyle and a lot on the mind makes listening very difficult.

To become a more attentive listener, here are some active listening techniques you could try.

- **Ask active listening questions like, "What I'm hearing is…" and "Sounds like you are saying…"** The occasional question or comment lets others know you're listening and helps you stay tuned in to them. In addition, it clarifies what they mean and prevents misunderstanding.

- **Don't prepare a rebuttal while the other person is talking.** Listen for the purpose of understanding, not for the purpose of interjecting your own experience. Remember that it's not necessary to "top" others' stories with a better one of your own.

- **Listen for the purpose of supporting others, not to find fault in them, correct them, or criticize them.**

- **They may not be asking for your opinion.** It might be that they only need to sort their feelings out loud, they want someone to understand where they are coming from, or they just want to be heard. It could be that they would like advice, but you must first determine if they are asking for the advice before you give it. Unwelcome advice comes across as judgmental. To be sure they want advice, ask, "Do you want my opinion and advice? Or do you just need to vent?"

- **Don't interrupt.** Interrupting another mid-sentence says you are done with what they have to say and are ready to enlighten them with your own thoughts. Interrupting is the opposite of being quick to listen.

The second part of this verse states we are to be "slow to speak." Do you know someone who talks way too much? When you picture this "talker," do you think of them as a wise person? Likely not, as it is impossible to gain insight when doing all the talking.

We don't stumble upon wisdom by chance. Wisdom is gained through the effort of listening to others. Some of us talk so much we miss the insightful gems of others' experiential wisdom. Let's not miss one opportunity to gain wisdom because we are busy with incessant chattering.

Discuss It: Do you think you do more of the talking or listening in conversations? Recall the last conversation you had with your spouse. Did you do more of the talking or more of the listening in that conversation? Which of the above active listening skills could you put effort into further developing?

Pray Over It: God, reveal to each of us whether we do more talking or listening. We pray you give us the ability to focus on each other, undistracted, without feeling the need to interject our own thoughts. May we value one another above ourselves and impress upon each other that we care and appreciate each other's words. Amen.

SLOW TO ANGER

My dear brothers, take note of this: Everyone should be
quick to listen, slow to speak and slow to become angry.

JAMES 1:19

In our society, we overload our schedules. We have a plethora of things to get done and an overabundance of concerns on our minds, causing us to become tightly wound. Then the little things, which normally don't bother us, prompt us to snap! We have been experiencing a stressful situation for several years. Joel gently pointed out to me that I had started snapping very quickly and easily over trivial things, whereas I hadn't lost my cool that easily in the past. I hadn't realized I was doing that. I had allowed myself to become wound too tightly.

Many times, if we're stressed about *anything*—even situations outside the home—it's our husband or wife who takes the brunt of our stress. We're mad the boss is expecting too much of us and we end up taking it out on the wife who let the garbage pile too high. Our kids aren't taking responsibility and we yell, instead, at the husband who ran late from work. This isn't fair to our spouse. If it's possible, we need to lighten our loads before we reach the point we're snapping. Whether or not we can remove our heavy burdens, we need to pay close attention to our tone, words, and attitude. Our calm and pleasant demeanors are so slippery, they're easy to lose when we're stressed.

"Snapping"—or losing control—is considered normal by some as if it's not possible to control the volcano inside. You can't always control the way things make you feel, but you do have complete control over your reactions. Have you ever been so angry that you "blew up" at someone, then your phone rang, and you suddenly gained control

187

of your anger, set it aside, and answered your phone with a polite greeting? This is because you do have control of yourself.

When we let our anger get in the way, rationality goes out the window. We are no longer thinking clearly and logically. Groucho Marx said, "If you speak when angry, you'll make the best speech you'll ever regret."[6] We have far more influence with others when we have a cool head and speak gently. When we're not in *attack-mode*, others aren't in *defense-mode* and are more willing to listen.

Let's apply James's advice to social media as well. Social media can get us so riled up. It's too easy to post a snappy reply, a harsh comment, or a huffy, snide remark. We can delete our harsh comments from social media, but not from someone's heart. It's a good idea to make it a practice never to post when angry. That might mean in a few minutes, but it could also mean a few days. If it really needs a reply, it can wait until we've had time to cool down. Once we've prayed about it, God may tell us to let it go. Sometimes, our best move is to remain silent, focus on the condition of our own heart and allow God to speak to the one who offended us. If their heart is open, God will speak to them at the right time and in the perfect way. If their heart isn't open, why do we think *we* could reach them?

Discuss It: Is there something that needs released from your busy schedule, so you're not so tightly wound? What circumstances cause you to "blow"? At a time when your stress was completely unrelated to your spouse, how might you have taken it out on him or her? What can you do to gain control over your anger before lashing out? How can you become more aware of your tone and the way you are coming across to others?

Pray Over It: God of Peace, show us where our schedules may need adjusted to allow us occasional times of serenity. Remind us to stop before we say something, or post something, out of anger. Help us to let go of the need to set people straight when they frustrate and anger us. Help us to be more aware of how we are coming across to others. We pray we can remain calm and peaceful when stressful events come our way. Give us self-control and may we not take our frustrations out on each other. Amen.

NOVEMBER

ENVY SAVAGE & BOASTING BEAST

*Love is patient, love is kind. It does not
envy, it does not boast, it is not proud.*

1 Corinthians 13:4

Envy and boasting—these two monsters are related. Envy growls, *You have it, but I want it.* Boasting roars, *I have it; don't you wish you did?* Both are ugly and need shown the door in our hearts.

The Greek word for *envy* means to eagerly desire and is rooted in greed and selfishness. Envy wants what others have, either tangible things like wealth, beauty, or a large house or intangible things like success, attention, admiration, a romantic relationship, an intact family, or the friendships others have. It is not wrong to desire such things. The disdain we feel toward others who have these things is wrong. If seeing others with something we lack causes us to feel slighted and upset, we have a problem with envy.

Envy looks different in a marriage because we own the same house, have the same wealth, go on the same vacations (typically), and share many of the same struggles. But sometimes we become jealous of our spouse's career, easier childhood, or lack of health problems. Maybe our spouse does not have the stresses that fall on us daily and we're feeling slighted.

Envy can, also, hurt our marriage when we envy another marriage that appears better and stronger than our own. Maybe we even envy another's spouse. Remember things aren't always as they appear. Every marriage goes through seasons. That beautiful marriage we admire may have recently risen out of a great struggle. Even if another

193

marriage has experienced less valleys than our own, jealousy helps nothing. We need to keep our focus on the good in our own marriage, little as it may be, and keep working toward improving it each day. What we focus on grows.

Love does not boast. The Greek word for *boast* describes someone who is full of himself and promotes himself, exaggerating to make himself look more important than others. The Greek word for *proud* is puffed up. While envy wants what others have, pride tries to make others jealous of what *we* have.

Boasters come in many varieties. There's the "low self-esteem" variety: those who have been broken in unhealthy places and need to prove their worth in unhealthy ways. They are afraid of the lies they've bought into about themselves. Though they might believe telling others impressive things about themselves will boost others' perception of them, in time, it has the opposite effect. Then there's the "personal gain" variety: those who attempt to gain higher position or authority through elevating themselves. Sometimes their boasting can appear innocent and subtle but it's boasting all the same. The "center stage" variety: these boasters are always throwing in a story to "top" others' experiences with a better story of their own. They manipulate the conversation to put themselves on center stage.

Most of us boast, at times, and struggle with pride. Most likely, we all can relate to at least one of these types of boasters. The truth is, we cannot love others well and boast at the same time. Boasting is centered on self, while love has concern for others.

Boasting is also not as obvious in a marriage, but it happens all the same. We may boast about how we were able to fix something the other could not. We may try to get our spouse to see us as superior—smarter, funnier, stronger, better looking. Oftentimes, we try to "top" our spouse's story, like, *What I went through was worse than that and, by the way, I could tolerate way more than you.* We may belittle our spouse, basically step on them, to rise above them.

How do we kill the monsters, envy and boasting? The best weapon? Contentment.

Envy dies when we find pleasure and serenity, both in what we have and in who we are. Instead of seeking "fairness," contentment brings us to genuine happiness for others' successes, possessions, and achievements, even if they are not ours to have. Realizing we don't need these things for fulfillment and holding gratitude for the things we do have, though it be significantly less, is the way to kill the beast of envy.

Contentment also kills boasting. When we are content in who we are, we can let our desire for others to view us as superior fall by the wayside. There's no need for boasting, no need to be viewed better than others.

Paul had learned to be content in every situation. For him, whatever he had was enough. In his words to the Philippians, he expressed his contentment, whether in plenty or in want, whether well-fed or hungry. He said the secret of being content was learned. It doesn't seem to be a coincidence he ends those thoughts with the famous phrase, "I can do all things through Christ who strengthens me" (Philippians 4:11-13 NKJV). Contentment empowers us to do all the things God has called us to.

When I (Joel) went on a mission's trip as a teenager, my mission's team attended a sort of "boot camp" to prepare us for the trip spiritually, mentally, and physically. There were multiple teams at this camp who were training for various missions. Every day we, as a team, had to compete in an obstacle course against all the other teams to reach the finish line the quickest. Here's the catch: The winner wasn't determined based on one person from each team making it to the finish line the quickest. Rather, it was determined by the first team to get every person on their team to cross the line. Our team was only as good as the weakest among us. So, we weren't simply focused on achieving our personal best, but on helping the ones who struggled to keep up. The lesson from this experience — the importance of teamwork — stuck with me through life and into my marriage. My marriage "team" can only go as far as the weakest among us. We are not competing against each other but competing as a team against "life."

We are not in a competition! We do not marry so that we have someone to outperform. Marriage is rising together as a team. Marriage is sharing in one another's joys and pain, even if we can take it better, even if we have better stories of our own.

So, when your spouse comes to you with a problem or an experience to share, it's the person in front of you, right there in that moment, that matters. That person wants to share this moment with you! Take that in. The privilege of sharing life with another is the prize you have won. Let that be enough.

Discuss It: Is there anything that makes you feel slighted when you see others have it? Which type of boaster can you most relate to — low self-esteem, personal gain, or center stage? How can you turn from these types of selfishness and pride? Is there anything your spouse has that makes you feel slighted? What needs to change for you to feel content with what you have? Name some tangible things you are grateful for. Name intangible things you are grateful for. What, in your marriage, are you grateful for? How can you focus more on these attributes throughout your day?

Pray Over It: Loving Father, sometimes we get this twinge in our hearts when we see something others have that we desperately desire. We pray you would transform our hearts, so we're genuinely happy for others instead of resentful. We don't want to have selfishness or any kind of pride. It was born along with us, and we need help fighting it every day. Strip away our pride and our need to impress others. Help us recognize when we're acting selfishly or trying to boost our approval rating with others. Remind us you love humility and help us to be content in all circumstances. We are thankful for [list out what you're grateful for]. We pray the good things in our marriage would expand and the weak parts of our marriage would strengthen. Amen.

THE HEALING POWER OF PLEASANT WORDS

Pleasant words are a honeycomb, sweet to the soul and healing to the bones.

PROVERBS 16:24 NASB

Words have incredible power—the power to make or break a relationship, a business, a family, a church, a marriage, and impressionable children. With just our words alone, we have the power to cause another to give up his dreams or to pursue them. We can cause a child to doubt herself by creating fear and apprehension, or we can give her the confidence to boldly lead those around her. We can cause our friends and spouse to give up in defeat or inspire them to accomplish what feels impossible.

Honey is both sweet and healing, as are our pleasant words to others. There have been times I (Mandy) felt as if I was failing but the words of another kept me going. Once in particular, I was going through a parenting rough patch. My kids' choices didn't reflect the way we raised them, and I felt defeated. Every day I'd wake up and wonder where I went wrong. I started to bite into Satan's lies that I was a failure of a mother. Then, a friend wrote me, out of the blue, telling me she thought I was a great mama. She said she could tell I had made many sacrifices for our children and had spent time training them right. She said she was impressed by the number of sacrifices I made for them. I can't tell you how sweet those words were to my soul, how healing to my weary bones!

Another instance of pleasant words healing to my bones was during my application for grad school, the Physician Assistant program.

I had studied and studied preparing for the GRE exam. After taking the test, I waited weeks for my grade, only to find out it wasn't good enough to get into the PA program. I was crushed. I felt defeat down to my core. I wanted to give up my dream of becoming a Physician Assistant right then and there, even though I had worked years to get to that point. I cried most of that day and went to bed feeling inadequate. The next day, I dragged myself out of bed and plodded down the stairs to find a sticky note at the bottom of the stairs that said, "You are loved." As I walked through the hallway, there was another note saying, "You are good enough." Feeling a little more confident, I walked into the bathroom to find another note on the mirror saying, "You are amazing!" As I walked into the kitchen to get my coffee, a dozen roses caught my attention. With the roses was a note saying, "Try it again. You can do this! Don't give up." Joel filled me with the pleasant words to heal my bones. I did try again a month later and got the grade I needed for grad school.

The world out there is tough enough. Home is, or should be, the place we are healed and recharged, the place we encounter the wind propelling us toward success. If we want to be this place for our spouse — a place to find healing from the beatings of the world, a place to refuel so they can keep grinding toward success — we create that space with our words.

Self-evaluation time: Think of the words that have come out of your mouth to your spouse over the past two days. Ask yourself, *Have my words conveyed understanding and compassion? Have my words made my spouse feel welcome to express himself or herself? Have my words further wounded? Have I come across as judging, critical, or cynical? How have my words healed my spouse from the beatings of this tough world? How have I contributed to the confidence he or she needs to keep going?*

Looking at ourselves and our own imperfections without immediately throwing up a defense is hard. But, for the sake of our spouse, let's take this self-evaluation honestly. It's hard to encourage another when we're feeling beat-down ourselves. But remember, by lifting others, we also rise.

One would think sweetening another's soul and bringing healing to their bones would take a lot more effort than just saying "pleasant words." Putting a new spring in another's step is as easy as saying, *You are amazing and here's why..., I believe you can do it..., If others haven't believed in you, they have been wrong, You inspire me to become a better person, You make me happy, I'm glad you're in my life, I need you, You have accomplished so much, You're stronger than you think...*

If we are critical by nature and generally short on "pleasant words," we need to recalibrate. If we ask God to give us the right words to encourage our spouse, he will do just that. We don't want to be the reason our spouse gives up a dream or walks around in defeat. We want to be the reason for his or her success.

Discuss It: Think of an instance when someone other than your spouse spoke sweet words to you at a time you needed them. Consider thanking them for that. Tell your spouse of a time his or her pleasant words were healing to your bones. Take the time to pour pleasant words into each other in this moment of discussion.

Pray Over It: God, thank you for the encouragement of others that keeps us going when we feel defeated. Help us to be aware of the words we say and how they will affect others. We pray we would be sensitive to each other's feelings and give one another the right words in the right moments. May our home be a place of healing. Amen.

A SPOONFUL
OF SUGAR

*Pleasant words are a honeycomb, sweet to
the soul and healing to the bones.*

Proverbs 16:24 NASB

When you think of election time coming, what feeling does that evoke in you? For most of us, it's anxiety as we're bombarded with the slanderous statements made by each candidate and their followers against those they oppose. The air is heavy with verbal assault, hatred, mudslinging, and slaughtering of reputations. It's just plain ugly. Where there once were fun-loving friendships, at election time, becomes friction and division.

So, do we just remain silent about issues that are important to us? Not necessarily. Mary Poppins enlightens us with wise advice, "Just a spoonful of sugar helps the medicine go down." The medicine (our words) has power, but the sugar (sweet words) makes it easier to swallow. Kind, gracious words accomplish far more than words spit out from a hateful heart. While angry words cause others' defenses to escalate, calm tones and words like, "I hear what you're saying, I respect your opinion, I can see why you think that… but I think…," go miles further.

This applies to marriage as well. No two people agree on every single topic. So, of course, we're going to have differences of opinion and disagreements now and then. It's okay to share our differences, as long as we're keeping love and respect in our words and tone.

The same is true for issues in other areas of our lives, within our families, our workplaces, and in the community. How about we make sure we're sweetening the medicine we want to go down? Let's pause before pouncing. Let's choose to hold that mighty tongue until emotions simmer down. Let's pray before we speak and ask God for the necessary measure of sweet honey. It's possible to prevent fights and subsequent deep wounds. Holding the tongue is easier than attempting to repair a relationship after the damage is done.

To take it further than prevention, let's be proactive and intentional about offering encouragement, support, good cheer, inspiration, and hope to others. During the mortgage meltdown of 2006, I (Joel) lost my business seemingly overnight. At that time, nobody was hiring, and I couldn't find another job to support the family. I wasn't making ends meet. I felt like a failure. However, Mandy spoke encouraging words over me. Even though the income was not enough, she made me feel like *I* was enough. Her pleasant words kept my spirit going through that hard time.

The power of pleasant words is immense. Let's start with our spouse and children, move on to the extended family, then spread it to social media and even to the strangers we run into. We never know just how badly someone needs to hear words "sweet to the soul" until we speak the "pleasant words" and watch their posture, life, and face brighten.

Discuss It: When was the last time you had to make amends because of hurtful words you said? Would it have been better if you had held your tongue instead? Consider a recent difference of opinion between you and your spouse. Practice using a kind tone and sweet words with your spouse (not sarcastic sweetness) to share your opinion and your reason for coming to that conclusion. Practice listening to your spouse with openness and respect.

Pray Over It: Father, make our words sweet like honey. Take away any desire we might have to lash out when we disagree or have been hurt. May we give pause to our angry thoughts and respond only after our anger has cooled. Give us your eyes to see the good in each other, the compassion to listen to each other, and the sweet words to speak to each other. Amen.

CONTENTMENT

*Keep your lives free from the love of money and be content
with what you have, because God has said, "Never
will I leave you; never will I forsake you."*

HEBREWS 13:5

Read this topic Scripture again. Does this make anyone else stop
and ask, *What do these two things have to do with each other—freedom from the love of money and God's promise to not leave or forsake us?*

What is the "love of money"? And why is Paul telling us to stay
free from it? Who doesn't love money? Am I sinning because I love
money?

The "love of money" has more to do with our hearts and less to
do with what we have. It's not wrong to enjoy what money can buy.
Sometimes, God decides to bless us with abundant wealth—take Job
for example. Physical blessings aren't wrong. What is wrong, even dangerous, is when we crave the satisfaction it brings, when we depend
on it to satisfy our hearts. It's to our detriment to believe wealth will
give us a sense of security, a sense of power, more options, or lavish
experiences. Desiring more and more is a trap that keeps us imprisoned. We need to work longer hours, get that promotion, change
careers. We're always chasing more and more money, and more and
more stuff. As soon as we get what we want, we're on to the next
thing we must have to bring us contentment. We want more than
our own hands can hold.

However, things disappoint. How many times have we bought
something we wanted—clothes or a new "toy"—and soon found
we didn't care for it anymore? Or invested a lot of money into a
new hobby that soon disinterested us? Everything we own—yes,

everything—will one day be in a dump. There are no exceptions. That gives a whole new perspective on things. When will we learn that nothing satisfies us for long?

What if we could have all those things—power, more options, lavish experiences—with a deeper relationship with God? It's possible, but not on our terms. The options, the experiences, the power, the security may not be the same as what we had in mind. It's a different kind of power, different options than we thought possible, and a different kind of experience, but richer and more satisfying for the soul. Furthermore, we don't have to change careers or work longer hours to get it.

Many of us have heard about the God-shaped hole inside each of us. Though we try to stuff things in there to fill it, they're the wrong shape. We will never be satisfied until we fill it with the precise thing that fits. Why did God even design that hole in us? Could it be that his desire to fill that space is just as strong, or stronger, than our desire to have it filled? He created us with a longing for him and he is passionately pursuing each of us. He longs for each one of us to allow him to quench our desires. Since he also created that hole in each of us, he alone knows exactly how to fill it, for it is the shape of him.

There is our answer. The reason those two things—freedom from the love of money and God's promise to never leave us—are put together in one verse. The love of money is the wrong shape. Our true contentment comes from God. He is with us, and that is enough. When we truly find contentment in him alone, we can come to a state of mind where we can say to God, *You can take away anything I have and I will be as content as I was before. I never really owned any of it anyway. It was always yours. You are enough for me.* That's the proof of authenticity. Can we say with Paul, "I have learned to be content whatever the circumstances. I know what it is to be in need, and I know what it is to have plenty. I have learned the secret of being content in any and every situation, whether well fed or hungry, whether living in plenty or in want"? (Philippians 4:11-12). That's deep down, soul-satisfying, rest-giving, heart-mending, peace-giving satisfaction. That is the place God wants us, the place he can use us the most. That is the place we will be most deeply satisfied in our innermost being.

We have a friend who always wanted pet birds but was held back from this dream because his wife didn't want them in the house. Sadly, this marriage ended in divorce — not over the birds, but other issues. But, with his wife no longer in his way, he finally got his birds. However, shortly afterward, he grew tired of them. He realized he didn't really like birds. They didn't bring him the satisfaction he thought they would. Let's remember this story when we feel unsatisfied with life and think it's our spouse keeping us from enjoying life the way we wanted.

Is dissatisfaction a point of contention in your marriage? Is your pursuit of obtaining material things causing dissension between you and your spouse? When your focus is on the eternal and you keep in mind everything you own will eventually be in a dump and nothing here satisfies forever, you begin to realize that bringing God glory through marital unity is of more value than any material thing. If your financial decisions are made from hearts contented by God, you will be more unified in those decisions, and God will be glorified.

Discuss It: What have you recently been dreaming of having? What would your life look like if that possibility were taken away from you? Would you be content? What do you own that, if taken from you, would bring you deep grief? Do you find it hard to trust God to content your heart? What steps could you take to fill all your desires with God alone? What areas in the budget do you, as a couple, disagree? (Don't argue about it now. Simply take it to God in prayer and then, later, seek outside advice.)

Pray Over It: God, thank you for all the good things you have given us [list them out]. We know that you are the one who provided all those things. Help us to hold our belongings loosely. We trust you with all of it. God, please reveal areas of our lives we feel unsatisfied. Fill us with so much contentment in you that we don't crave anything else. Help us to maintain a heavenly perspective as we make financial decisions together. May we show one another love and respect by the way we spend our money. Amen.

DECEMBER

LOVING WITH UNSELFISH MOTIVES

If I speak in the tongues of men or of angels, but do not have love, I am only a resounding gong or a clanging cymbal. If I have the gift of prophecy and can fathom all mysteries and all knowledge, and if I have a faith that can move mountains, but do not have love, I am nothing. If I give all I possess to the poor and give over my body to hardship that I may boast, but do not have love, I gain nothing.

1 CORINTHIANS 13:1-3

A rampage of persecution was sweeping through the church at the time of Paul's writing to the Corinthian people, and to this day still rages on in some parts of the world. There were some early Christians who thought their suffering, especially death by martyrdom, was the most important part of being a Christian. But Paul taught them about the importance and priority of love—that without it, nothing is gained. Not only do we gain nothing, we *are* nothing, without love. Love is the absolute most important thing—so important, any sacrifice we make is of no value without it.

In a prior devotion, we learned the Greek word for *love* used in 1 Corinthians 13 is *agape*. To recap, agape love is self-sacrificing love. It gives without demands or self-serving expectations. It's given without pride or desire for recognition. It has little to do with the fuzzy feeling of love and much to do with self-denial for the sake of another. Agape love is uncorrupted by selfish motives.

How can we love with such purity? Agape love is awakened when we realize God's love for us, when we remember that though we may break God's heart, we'll never break his love for us or our worth to him. It's from this full-hearted place we can express genuine love for others. Who are we to accept God's love and refuse love to others?

When it comes to agape love, we think of those who had nothing to gain from what they forfeited. Take for example, Owen and Charlotte, who downsized their house and vacation budget so they would be free to give to any need brought to their awareness. We think of those in our small group, who gave up a Saturday to clean and paint a children's group home. We think of our friend, Lia, who gently steers conversations away from gossip to protect those being gossiped about, even those who have hurt her. We think of Roger, who fights his depression and gets out of bed every day with a forced smile because his family needs him. We think of Faith who makes it a habit to pay for the orders of the people in the car behind her in the drive-through line even though her budget is small.

When we think of martyrs, we are so moved by their faith and unswerving commitment to God, we put them on a pedestal—and rightly so! They made the ultimate sacrifice, absolutely everything, including their own earthly lives. But Paul taught us that *anything* done in love, through self-sacrifice without thought of personal gain, no matter how small, is more important than *anything* done for accolades or our own personal gain no matter how grand.

Sometimes this agape love, selfless and sacrificial without expectations, is necessary to keep a marriage going. What does agape love look like in a marriage?

- Serving our spouse even after our hearts were broken by them.

- Choosing not to bring up past wrongs.

- Loving with no strings attached—strings like doing the dishes she usually does for the purpose of getting some action in bed or giving in bed with intentions to get him to work on that honey-do list.

- Giving a back rub with no expectation of a returned massage.

- Offering grace when they came home late with no notice or apologies.

- Turning down a high-paying job that comes with status but requires much time away from home and, instead, choosing the job that meets a minimum budget but renders plenty of time for family and marital connection.

- Running to the store in the middle of the night to get them medicine or that food they've been craving.

- Letting go of "being right" and "I told you so."

- Listening without interjecting personal opinions and advice.

- Asking for their advice, even at a time we really don't care.

- Cheering them on even though our own dreams weren't supported.

- Protecting their reputation even when they've hurt us.

- Cheerfully allowing them to spend a little extra on their hobby, though their hobby brings us no pleasure.

- Showing respect through our words and tone even when we don't admire their recent decisions.

- Serving them with gratitude instead of grumbling.

- Remaining humble, open, and teachable rather than defensive.

- Continuing to serve them when no appreciation has been given.

- Praying good things for their life.

If we ask ourselves, *Am I doing this to get something in return?* and our answer is *Yes,* then we have ulterior motives, and our spouse has become a business transaction instead of a lifelong companion.

How can we do these things? How can we keep showing love when it's not being returned? It's not possible on our own. Agape love can only be given by tapping into God's agape love for us. We need to pray and ask God for more. He is happy to give. Recall God's agape love for us, reflect on his goodness, and remember loving others is how we love God in return. Our mindset shifts from *doing it for man* to *doing it for God,* one little act at a time. Marriage gives us plenty of opportunities to practice!

According to Paul, love surpasses all the gifts we have, all the genuine good we do (gifts, prophecy, knowledge, and faith) and all the insincere good we do (giving with impure motives and suffering for the purpose of receiving admiration). This is pure love. This is our calling.

Discuss It: Can you think of a time you made a sacrifice, but its purpose was to gain something—admiration, an upward climb for the career, a false kindness with hopes of getting something in return? What gifts or talents have you been given that you could use to love God and others? How could you use that gift with no expectations of personal gain? Answer this next question introspectively: As you read through the ways agape love can be demonstrated in your marriage, what struck a chord in you? When you serve your spouse, consider shifting your perspective to God as the recipient.

Pray Over It: God, thank you for offering us your unconditional, sacrificial love. May we remember that always and, in turn, pass that on to family, friends, and one another. Show us the gifts and sacrifices you would have us offer. We pray our gifts would not be wasted and used only for suiting our own personal desires. Help us to remember we have nothing, and *are* nothing, without love. May we seize the opportunities you put in front of us to love genuinely. Amen.

THE ADVANTAGE OF OVERLOOKING INSULTS

*Fools show their annoyance at once, but
the prudent overlook an insult.*

PROVERBS 12:16

Sometimes we argue over the pettiest things. Although we—Joel and Mandy—have had some major disagreements over some crucial topics, some of our most heated debates have been over the most trivial things. The most heated and shallow argument that comes to mind was over closet space. Yes, who got how much of the closet! Instead of "showing annoyance at once," could this argument have been contained if one of us had "overlooked the insult" of the other's accusations of greed because they allowed their clothes to take over? Would things have gone better had we allowed things to cool before discussing this minor annoyance civilly? Absolutely.

Before we dive further into this devotion, it's important to clarify it is not suggested to "overlook" verbal abuse, turn a blind eye, and become a doormat for future abuse. This devotion is addressing bickering and our timing with "showing annoyance." Statements like, *Of course, he's running to you and crying dramatically over a minor scratch because you baby him.* Or a disrespectful eye roll when our spouse shares his or her feelings.

These issues of disrespect *should be* addressed. Our spouse should know how their words are hurting us, but quickly spouting off a snappy, rude retort is only the kick-off to an unproductive bickering session. If we were to, instead, address issues later with a cool, calm tone, we would then have a healthy, more productive conversation. Not showing annoyance "at once" means we will address it when the environment and emotions have calmed.

By withholding a snappy, emotional response, we can stop the back-and-forth bickering in its tracks. Holding back a counterattack shows great strength — more strength than the knee-jerk reactions that typically fly out of our mouths. The mature person responds to insults cautiously, knowing the power he holds — power to either take the heat out of the moment or allow the situation to go down in flames.

Another example of withholding "showing annoyance at once" is when our spouse is not hurting us, only getting under our skin, and it's a petty thing causing our upset. Maybe we're not a morning person and our spouse likes to sing cheerily in the mornings. Or maybe our spouse tells cheesy jokes that annoy us. We need to give room for our spouse to be who he or she is. We need to release our desire to change our spouse. Remember we said, "I do," not "I re-do."

In marriage, our quick responses have incredible power to set the direction of a simple disagreement or, after developing into habit, to set the direction of our entire marriage. Often, our responses have repercussions long into the future, whether positive or negative. Are we going to address our annoyances later when emotions have cooled and take the marriage in the direction of strength, trust, and security? Or spew out a quick retort when emotions are high and allow the marriage move toward insecurity, dysfunction, and despair? One small response at a time eventually impacts the lifetime of the marriage.

This applies, not just to marriage, but to other areas of life as well. In the workplace, responding to an insult may create drama, giving the impression to our boss and coworkers that we are neither professional nor a good team member. Among family or friends, we can allow for a hostile environment, or choose to diffuse tension by letting spiteful comments roll off. In parenting, training children is more fruitful when negative emotions aren't displayed by the parent. Anger and yelling increase the child's anxiety which is not an optimal state for children to learn.

So how do we control the tongue when we feel our blood start to boil? Here are some simple ways, in the heat of anger, to tame the rabid dog clawing its way out of our mouths:

- **Deep breaths.** According to multiple studies, deep breathing increases the supply of oxygen to the brain, stimulates the parasympathetic nervous system, and promotes a state of calm. Take in a deep breath, then let it out slowly. Repeat.

- **Don't sweat the small stuff.** Don't give the minor stressors a room for rent in your head. Evict 'em! Save your headspace for the thoughts worthy of your attention.

- **In that very brief moment of deciding how to respond, envision a good outcome, then consider what needs to happen to get to that point.**

- **Keep your esteem dependent on God.** The one who is not consumed with proving his worth to others is the one who can ignore the insult. A truly humble person is not thinking of himself at all, but instead concerned about pleasing God alone. That person who truly understands he is the one Jesus would "leave the ninety-nine" for is the person with no need for a sharp retort to prove his worth.

Not only can we contain the back-and-forth bickering, we can contain the hurt within our hearts. We can prevent those insults from eating away at us. Sometimes we let the harsh, hurtful words settle into our souls, inviting them to destroy us on the inside. But it would do us well to block the insults from reaching our heart and, instead, touch base with God for our worth.

Discuss It: In what area of life do you allow others to get a rise out of you—with family, at work, while driving, in parenting? Consider ways to keep the situation from escalating, both in your outward response and in your heart regarding your self-worth. Is there a petty annoyance you have toward a behavior of your spouse that's not hurting you? In what area of life do you quickly show your annoyance? What recent situation could have ended better if you had chosen to let it go? Which of the above listed ways of taming the tongue will you begin working on today?

Pray Over It: Father, forgive us for allowing our emotions to rule our responses. Bring healing to the areas of our lives we have ruined with our angry retorts. Though we don't have control over some situations, we do have control of many by our responses which decide the direction of our lives and our marriage. We pray your gentleness would rule in our lives. May we not be known as hot-tempered individuals with quick, hurtful retorts, but as wise people who use discretion with our words. Help us to be cautious and controlled when we feel rage welling inside. Help us be peacemakers in our workplaces, with our family, while driving, and with our kids. May we let hurtful comments roll off and depend only on you for our worth. You hold us in high regard, and we pray we can fully grasp what that means. Amen.

A SHELTER
FOR OTHERS

It always protects, always trusts, always hopes, always perseveres.

1 CORINTHIANS 13:7

ove always protects. The word *protect* in Greek is *stego*, which means to protect by covering, in the way a roof covers a house and protects from bad weather. Like a roof, our love is a shelter over others from the hailstorms beating them up. *Stego* protects others not only physically by providing for their tangible needs, but emotionally and spiritually as well. It supports their need to belong, upholds their character and reputation, and brings them closer to Jesus. Love that always protects looks out for the one who may not feel valued or included. It doesn't go around updating people of the problems of others or sharing things spoken in confidence (Proverbs 17:9). It does not deflate others with painful sarcasm and put-downs or make jokes at another's expense. Love defends the character of others whenever it can, even when that person isn't around — *especially* when that person isn't around to defend him or herself. It's easy to jump in and agree when someone's dirty laundry is aired behind his or her back, especially if we, too, have been hurt by that person. What if instead, we defended that person by jumping in with the benefit of the doubt? Usually there's a back story we don't know and the one "in question" is doing the best they know how at that moment, with cards in hand of which we are unaware. Wouldn't we want others to give *us* the benefit of the doubt and come to our defense when we're not around? It comes down to grace. Just as God's grace protects us, so are we to protect others with grace.

Love always trusts. This means believing the best in every person and situation. Love is not suspicious and doubting of the other person's character and motives without good reason. Love believes others are innocent until proven guilty, not the other way around. This does not mean we naïvely abandon all discernment. It means the benefit of the doubt is given before accusation; we don't rush to believe the worst. If a problem arises, love doesn't jump immediately to blame the other person. Not that trust shouldn't be earned back once broken, but love hopes that trust can and will be restored, and gives it the opportunity to be earned back, even if with a guarded heart. It's not constantly singing the "Remember When You Broke My Heart Reprise." It's not gripping resentment, preventing trust from ever having a chance of being regained. Love always trusts, or hopes to trust, again.

As a husband or wife, we are to be a *stego*, protection, for our spouse. As a roof covers and shelters from the rain, we protect our spouse's reputation and make him or her feel valued. This means we are coming to their defense when they are insulted. We're not talking bad about them to fuel other people's anger toward them. We aren't making jokes about them or ridiculing them. In fact, we are doing the exact opposite and pouring into them compliments, encouragement, and our admiration.

When we are hurt by our spouse, we tend to shut them out of our hearts to protect us from further pain. It's wise to guard our hearts from further hurt and pain, to "test the waters" slowly, and require proof of change before letting down our guard. But, if we love with trust, we don't completely shut the door to reconciliation. We, instead, continue to hope for the best in our spouse and keep the possibility of restoration open. We aspire to, one day, come back stronger than ever.

Discuss It: Can you think of a time you didn't give someone the benefit of the doubt, came to a judgement about them, then later learned your judgement was inaccurate? Outside of marriage, in what relationships do you feel you have not protected another the way you should have? How could you better support the character of your co-workers? Family members? Friends? Whom have you shut out from your heart due to broken trust? Could you give them opportunity to earn back your trust? If your spouse has hurt you in the past and you have shut an area of your heart to him or her, pray for direction with re-opening your heart.

Pray Over It: Lord, thank you for teaching us what real love looks like. Help us to understand the responsibility you have placed on us to protect those you've put in our lives. We pray we would always give grace when we don't have all the details. Help us, with healthy boundaries in place, to hope for repaired trust in our broken relationships. Help us to speak about each other in a way that is honoring and to pour life and encouragement into each other. Help us to keep the door open for reconciliation, always. Amen.

HANG ON & HOPE

It always protects, always trusts,
always hopes, always perseveres.

1 CORINTHIANS 13:7

Love always hopes. Hope is the full anticipation that good will rise up. It keeps pushing through defeat to get to that ultimate success. Hope does not dwell on past dead-ends but looks forward to the future with confidence and faith in God's ability. This is not a false sense of reality, but a resting on God's promise that he is working all things together for good. This hope knows God can move mountains and, also, trusts he has a better plan if he chooses to leave those mountains in place.

The opposite of this hope is pessimism. Think of a pessimist in your life who sees only the worst possible outcomes, notices only the flaws in people, does not explore options to overcome his or her circumstances, and complains of being stuck. These pessimists are even annoyed by others who see the bright side of things. They are killjoys, bringing out the worst in everyone. Now think of an optimist in your life who chooses to focus on the good, counts their blessings, encourages others, brings out the best in everyone, and explores ways to better situations. With which person would you rather spend a day? Which person is making strides toward making the world a better place? Which person do you want to be? It all starts with the way you view the world. A gloomy outlook does not thrive in a heart full of hope.

My brother-in-law, a successful businessman, said when he's in a difficult situation, he pictures a good outcome. Then he thinks about the steps it will take and the things he will need to say (or not say), to get to that outcome. It almost always works out favorably for him with his optimistic hope. In the same way, when a husband and wife are filled with hope and they choose to foresee a good outcome in their marriage, the steps they will take lead to a marriage that thrives.

Love always perseveres. *Persevere* here means to take on the assault of an enemy without surrender. It is carrying a heavy load but refusing to let it defeat us. It means hanging in there when the going gets tough and people become hard to love. We tend to bail out when we've grown weary, the situation becomes complicated, or people become hard to love. Many times, if we don't like something petty that happens in a church, we go find another church. If a friend lets us down, we discard the friendship. We find things getting stale in the marriage, so we look for the pizazz we crave elsewhere.

A healthy marriage has mountaintops, plateaus, and valleys. Sometimes deep, dark valleys. However, the marriage becomes stronger when we climb from the valley back to the mountaintop together. But growing stronger together requires perseverance. It means we "take on the assault of the enemy without surrender" to reach that peak once again. We forgive, stick it out, and work toward better days with fierce determination.

A healthy marriage isn't two perfect people living together in perpetual bliss. It's two very imperfect people dealing with one another's imperfections according to perfect love. It's holding on when the road gets bumpy because we know God is up to some great things when we hang on. When we say, "I'm not quitting. I'm here to stay," God often blesses us with something more beautiful than we originally had. Recall the rewards God gave when Abram and Sarai waited for a child and when Job stuck with God through his trials. It's through the climb—through persevering—we gain strength.

(Side Note: There are times a marriage becomes corroded with abuse or adultery. These are not the instances where God is asking us to persevere. Please seek professional counsel if you are in this situation.)

Discuss It: Is there a relationship you gave up when you could have persevered? How could you have applied the truth concerning godly love, hope, and perseverance to those situations and relationships? Do you tend to be pessimistic about the future or do you hope for the best outcome and trust God will create beauty from ashes? Think of a current disagreement between you and your spouse. Discuss what you picture would be a good outcome for this situation.

Pray Over It: God of Hope, help us to look for the good in our situations and to anticipate the good in others. Give us the strength we need to persevere with fierce determination in the areas we're lacking stick-to-it-iveness. Please lift our struggling relationships from the valleys and boost them to the mountaintops. Help us to hold on tightly to hope and to persevere in our marriage. Amen.

CONCLUSION

On this journey through Scripture together, we hope you grew closer to God and deepened your relationship with your spouse like never before. This book of couples' devotions is a just one part of the whole package for Marriage In Abundance's approach to a better marriage. Also available are date plans to foster quality time together and marriage challenges to bring intentionality to the marriage, rekindling the romance. If you are not already participating in the full package of Marriage In Abundance, find out how at www.marriageinabundance.com.

Here's to a better marriage!

> If you liked these devotions, Mandy Shrock's book, *Life In Abundance,* contains some of the same devotions contained here in *Marriage In Abundance's Devotions for Married Couples*, but is intended for anyone, no matter their stage in life. *Life In Abundance,* also, has devotions not contained here—twice the amount of devotions—meant for deepening your personal relationship with God and improving your relationships.

APPENDIX

A NOTE TO HUSBANDS FROM JOEL

THE RESPONSIBILITIES OF THE HUSBAND

Relationships are not always easy. Marriages are full of conflict and prove to be very challenging at times. Throughout the ages, the look of marriage has changed over time. However, it's helpful to know Scripture, the foundation of our spiritual lives and God's expressed desires for our lives, teaches about marriage and is lasting and relevant throughout times — even through changing times. The longest passage in the Bible regarding marriage relationships is in Ephesians 5:22-33. Here, we see three verses directed toward wives, but nine verses are for the husbands. This could give some indication as to how much weight we husbands bear in cultivating our marriages.

Let's explore this passage for us husbands, verse by verse. Starting in verse 25, we read, "Husbands, love your wives, just as Christ loved the church and gave himself up for her." It's important to note, Christ gave himself up for the church. Literally, he gave up his life. But also, he died to himself and his own desires daily. He served others — washed feet, fed thousands, and stopped what he was doing to heal. When we love our wives like Christ loves the church, this means we are also dying to our own desires daily. Other than jumping in front of a bullet for her or pushing her out of the way of a runaway train and bearing the impact ourselves, more practically speaking, we carry her burdens, serve her, and make her our main priority. Some simple examples of giving up our lives for her: giving up a sports game to do something we know she's been wanting to do, grabbing her a coffee when we grab one for ourselves, considering her in our decisions, giving more time to dating her than guys' night or golfing, talking to her about the details of our day—even when we just want to veg out. The essence of Christianity is to put others above ourselves. This means our wives, too.

For us men, this can be a vulnerable area. *What if she doesn't even notice I'm choosing her above everything else? What if she doesn't treat me with respect? What if she makes me feel insignificant? What if she only takes, without reciprocating?* In 1 John 4:19, we read Christ loved us first before we loved him. God didn't wait until we were perfect, until we understood, until we even accepted him before he died for us. So, mirroring Christ's love for us, we are to exemplify the selflessness of Christ and be willing to put ourselves out there on the line.

Taking it a bit deeper, we are commanded to do everything for the glory of God (1 Corinthians 10:31). And Jesus says in Matthew 25:40, we should serve others as if we are serving him. This means how we serve our wife is not dependent on her attitude toward us. We are serving our God—putting ourselves out there on the line daily by serving our wife—no matter her response. We do it for God.

Let's say we want a garden containing vegetables worthy of grilling on a skewer. We would work hard, dominate those weeds, and end up with our best produce to enjoy. Likewise, if we want to enjoy a great marriage, we must be willing to work hard at it and conquer any problems that arise to give the marriage life.

Moving on to the next part. Verses 26-27 say husbands should, "make her holy, cleansing her by the washing with water through the word, and to present her to himself as a radiant church, without stain or wrinkle or any other blemish, but holy and blameless." This is a great picture of how God himself views us, his bride. But how do we do this—make her holy, cleanse her, present her blameless before the Lord? Romans 12:2 tells us to be transformed by renewing our minds and then gives practical advice for how we can accomplish this in verses 9-21. Taking the principles of Romans 12 and applying them to our relationship with our wives, it looks like cultivating a house of peace, sharing our own struggles with her, praying for and with her, reminding her of God's numerous promises for her in Scripture, guarding her against spiritual attacks, finding joy with her, being there for her when she's upset or grieving, acting with humility in our relationship with her, letting go of the urge to get back at her when we've been wronged. As husbands, we should be striving to cultivate our wife's spiritual growth and holiness.

Verses 28-30 say, "In this same way, husbands ought to love their wives as their own bodies. He who loves his wife loves himself. After all, no one ever hated their own body, but they feed and care for their body, just as Christ does the church—for we are members of his body." In addition, Genesis 2:24 talks about us becoming "one flesh." Thinking of our wives as one unit—an extension of our own body—we will love and care for her as we love and care for our own body.

Admittedly, I tend to get "hangry" when I haven't eaten for a while. In those moments, I will consume whatever is in sight to feed the mad stomach. I don't disregard my body's need, and I don't get mad at my stomach for having that need. I simply take care of my body's needs when I recognize the signal.

If we're loving and taking care of our wife as we love and take care of our own bodies, as husbands, we must train ourselves to look out for our wife's needs, not disregard the needs, not get mad at her for having that need for love and attention. Afterall, when we've planted something that we want to harvest, we must cultivate the soil and tend to the needs of the plant. Showing affection to our wife is like fertilizing our favorite garden.

Women are multipliers. When a woman is given something good, she returns it better. But give her something bad, and it will be returned more bitter. This is not to say it is justified for a woman to return negativity. That's not God's way, but the way of our sinful nature. Relationships, made of imperfect people, are not all idyllic. Many times, there has been hurt and damaged trust in the marriage. It may not be our fault if we put in the effort and it's not reciprocated, but we shouldn't provoke our wives unfairly or knowingly push her buttons. We should work toward giving the good as our go-to response. In this way, we will be serving God in our part of the marriage, and we will more likely get back the good in surplus.

You may be thinking, I want to love her, serve her, and nourish her emotionally, but I don't know how to practically apply it in everyday life. That's where we come in! Our goal is to help you cultivate that. At Marriage In Abundance, we provide you with simple ideas, marriage challenges, once a week to pursue her, reignite the spark, and draw you closer together. Ideas such as: while she's doing the dishes, kiss her cheek and tell her to go sit down while you finish them, notice the details of her hard work and thank her for it, surprise her by grabbing her favorite snack on your way home from work, or hug her and whisper in her ear one of the reasons you fell for her. If you would like to receive weekly marriage challenges, go to www.marriageinabundance.com to learn how you can participate.

Paul tells us in Romans 12:18 that as much as it depends on us, we should live at peace with one another. So, give your wife your best, whether she deserves it or not, because you are doing it for God. Work for the relationship you want to have that bears good fruit. And remember, people take time to trust, grow, and bloom. Changing your actions and reactions to her won't fix things in one day. The marriage garden takes a lifetime of cultivation. Using the old gardener's rule of thumb, new plants will first sleep, creep, then leap. Like a tended garden, patience and persistence will make your marriage leap!

A NOTE TO WIVES FROM MANDY

Wives, submit yourselves to your own husbands as you do to the Lord. For the husband is the head of the wife as Christ is the head of the church, his body, of which he is the Savior. Now as the church submits to Christ, so also wives should submit to their husbands in everything.

EPHESIANS 5:22-24

THE "S" WORD – SUBMISSION

From one woman's heart to another, let's dig into this sensitive subject together—submission. This word drudges up all kinds of feelings in us women, usually negative. Maybe we picture a Tarzan-like figure beating or threatening a woman into becoming a doormat for him, commanding her to cater to him silently as if her opinions are worthless and she is nothing more than a slave to him. What an awful image! This image is on one end of the spectrum, while on the other end, we have women dismissing the command to submit, saying it's outdated in the light of the progress in women's rights movements.

If the concept of submission was ever painted in a negative light, it was painted wrong. My hope is to shed a positive light on that "S" word and ignite in you a new desire to carry out this idea into your marriage. I want to help you appreciate it as the high calling that it is.

Scripture is clear about the roles of husbands and wives, stating multiple times for wives to submit to their husbands (Colossians 3:18, Titus 2:5, 1 Peter 3:5, Ephesians 5:22). It seems to me God means business in this department. Why would this be important to God?

Imagine two referees, both completely capable of calling shots but seeing plays from different angles. Picture what would happen if they were both calling the shots over the same plays. It wouldn't work. Chaos would ensue. As we know God is the God of peace. Therefore, within the family unit, God set up an order for peace to rule to obtain some sense of unity. If ever a decision were called into question, God clears up the confusion by having a system of order in place. Submission was never meant to cause any of us suffering. Its purpose is peace and unity.

One way to destroy a unit, whether it's a military unit or a family unit, is to create division among the ranks. Satan used this strategy in the Garden of Eden when he went to Eve first and convinced her to question Adam's leadership. He is still using this tactic today to convince women their happiness is found in usurping her husband's authority. Friends, by disrespecting our husbands, we are being played for a fool!

Though women have faced subjugation by men through the ages, women's rights are at an all-time high here in the United States, and for that I am grateful! Women are equal in value and deserve equal rights in society. However, in a marriage, God grants us different roles for the sake of unity. Unfortunately, many Christians are confusing women's rights in society, which is a good thing, with equal roles within a marriage. Although God created us equal in worth, we were created with different bodies, different qualities, varying abilities, and different roles. The husband and wife have qualities that vary but complement one another fantastically.

Before we dive in to discuss exactly what submission is — the meaning and application of it — let's discuss what submission is *not*.

Submission is not derogatory. God isn't asking us wives to do anything Jesus himself wasn't willing to do. Jesus submitted himself to the Father's will for the purpose of conquering evil. Husbands and wives were created as a reflection of the relationship between the Father and Son — equal in value and significance, but each having different roles — for the purpose of conquering evil (Genesis 1:26-27).

The Bible also compares marriage to the relationship between Christ and the Church. Christ never submits to the Church. Although he considers her needs and even sacrificed himself for her, Christ takes the leading role, and the Church follows suit.

The husband is granted a type of authority within a marriage, but he's not off the hook to lead however he feels. Authority granted by God is never for the purpose of building up the one in authority but to protect and bless those under the authority. In fact, those in authority have great responsibility and will be judged by God based on how they used their authority. Scripture certainly doesn't make it easy for him as he's given some heavy instructions on how to lead. Every time the Bible encourages wives to submit to their husbands, it is followed up with further instruction for the husband to not abuse his authority but to use it to lead with love (Colossians 3:18-19, Titus 2:5-8, 1 Peter 3:5-7, Ephesians 5:22-30). The husband is commanded to love his wife, to not be harsh with her, and to serve her. He is to love her as he loves himself (which may be a pretty big deal!), be understanding with her, care for her, show her honor, and give himself up for her. He is to lead her without self-seeking motives. Both the husband and the wife were given responsibility to one another, and neither command is easy. Servanthood and sacrifice remain mutual while still preserving the leadership role to the husband.

If your husband is a power-hungry alpha male type and not concerned about your well-being, guard yourself. If he is harming you, you obey a greater command and do what you need to do to protect your mind, body, and spirit. If you are in this situation, please seek safety and counseling. This article is written to address situations in which the safety of those involved is not endangered.

Another thing submission is *not*: it is not meant for the wife to simply do everything her husband tells her without question, without discussion. Remember, there are two capable refs out on the field who need to confer what they're seeing on the field with one another. One may see a play at an angle the other didn't see or bring wisdom from past experience, which reveals further insight to the current situation. Relationships are built on honesty and, along with that, comes honesty with feelings as well. If a wife feels her husband is making a choice that will have negative consequences, she should speak up.

Her feelings are valid and withholding them from him only creates distance in the relationship.

Submission does not forcibly impose obedience. Wives are not powerless. Submission means "surrender one's will." Surrendering is an active role. It is something she does, not something that is taken away from her. The one who voluntarily gives up her will to maintain God's order for peacekeeping is, in effect, in a place of power as she has the choice to give it up or not give it up. Jesus never forces our submission, but lovingly requests it.

Another thing submission is *not* is a command for *all* women to submit to *all* men. To add clarity to Scripture, the only references in the Bible for a woman to submit her will is within a marriage. God values women and uses them in leadership positions. In fact, many times in the Bible, God placed a woman in a position of leadership among men. God would not, *could not*, do something that goes against his own heart. Yet, God appointed Deborah as a judge—a position of high authority—over all of Israel (Judges 4). He chose many female prophets to speak his Word to men: Miriam (Exodus 15:20), Huldah (2 Kings 22:14-15), Anna (Luke 2:36) and Philip's daughters (Acts 21:8-9). There is an argument that God chooses women to lead only when men are unavailable, but this cannot be supported by Scripture. Furthermore, we need to be careful that we are not suppressing God's voice—putting God in a box—when God chooses a woman as his voice.

Submission is *not* just for women. In Christian culture, both men and women submit in many different forms to others: to be peacemakers, to forgive, to respect authority, to go the extra mile, and to give others more than is asked. Christianity is about dying to "self" to bring God to light. When we do take a stand, it is not for personal gain but only for the glory of God. So, it makes sense that wives would be encouraged to set aside their wills, at times, as this is not a foreign concept in Christianity.

We've thoroughly covered what submission is *not*. Let's dig into what it *is*. Submission, for us as wives, is a call to yield to our husband's leadership, to have regard for his decisions, and to support him in carrying them out. It means we don't kick and scream over his calls on the plays as the head referee. God created some of us with a fiery passion and he did it for a reason. That fiery passion can be a good thing! Our fiery spirit may even be the reason our husband loves us so much. But there are times to unleash our fiery passion and times to rein it in. The time after conferring with one another, when the final call is announced, is the time to rein it in. A good leader of a husband will take his wife's thoughts into consideration and pray before making his final decision. If his final decision doesn't go against Scripture, she should not argue and she should even take it a mile further by offering her support in carrying out his decisions.

Submission is an act of worship just as much as any other act. Worship includes singing praises, serving others, giving sacrificially and, also, submitting our wills to the greater good. As wives, we do not submit to our husbands for our husband's sake, but for God's sake, as an act of obedience to our Sovereign Father. Our hope is not in our husband, it is in God. And by obeying God, we are releasing our will *not* for the will of our husband but for the glory of God. We keep our minds steadfast on Kingdom goals until the world's goals are dimmed.

Generally, when someone notices a problem, they have a desire to fix it. As wives, we are in a position where we see problems most evidently. Who more deeply knows a man than his wife? As wives, we best see his flaws and, naturally, we want to fix his flaws. But we are never called to such duties. In fact, we may only be getting in God's way when we attempt to "fix" our husbands. True submission leaves his improvement journey open for God to work. When we take control, we are telling God we don't trust he will work it out and bring good into every situation. It's our obedience that allows God to be God; only he can change a heart. How ironic this is: Scripture says the best way for a wife to "change" her husband is *not* through trying to overpower his decisions, but by praying, swerving out of the way, and watching God change him.

God's ways are often paradoxical. They don't always make sense to our ways. If we knew all the thoughts of God and the intricacies of him, we would have no need to seek him. But we lack something—something God has—which is why we seek him. His ways are higher than our ways. It is beneficial to us to trust the one who made us, the one who knows us, the one who designed the family unit, the one who knows best how it operates, the one who calls us wives to obedience and submission, as he himself in his bodily form was willing to do.

God rewards our acts of faith. First Peter 1:6-7 says the genuineness of our faith will be tested, and the result will be praise, glory, and honor. Submitting our wills to another is a complete act of faith, and it, too, will be rewarded.

Submission is a high calling. It is not for the faint-hearted. It takes a strong woman to set aside her desires. It's this strength—this fiery passion under control—that brings beauty to the ruler of it. There is something alluring to the calming of the will and the peace that diffuses throughout difficult situations. Picture a woman trying to control a man versus a woman having regard for her husband's wishes, though her desire is elsewhere. There is beauty within the "S" word. The husband sees it and God sees it. Submission is, between the husband and wife, a beautiful dance.

NOTES

1. Crowe, Cameron. *Jerry Maguire*. TriStar Pictures, 1996.

2. Susan Cheever, *A Woman's Life: The Story of an Ordinary American and Her Extraordinary Generation*, (New York: William Morrow and Company, 1994), 132-133.

3. Erickson, Thane M., et al. "Compassionate and Self-Image Goals as Interpersonal Maintenance Factors in Clinical Depression and Anxiety." *Journal of Clinical Psychology*. 74. 12 September 2017: 608-628. Epub. 27 June, 2022. https://pubmed.ncbi.nlm.nih.gov/28898407/

4. Van Dyke, Mikella. "HELPMATE the REAL meaning of the word." Chasing Sacred, Accessed July 27, 2022, https://www.chasingsacred.com/helpmate-the-real-meaning-of-the-word/

5. West, Kanye. Interview. Conducted by Sway in the Morning. 26 November, 2013.

6. Starr, Eve. "Inside TV." *Greensboro Record*, Greensboro, North Carolina. November 4, 1954, Page B3, Column 4. GenealogyBank.

ABOUT THE AUTHORS

Joel and Mandy Shrock have been married over twenty years and have four kids. Together, they share a passion for marriage. Joel has taught marriage classes and Mandy has written marriage curriculum designed to breathe new life into marriages. They have led marriage retreats and mentored others through seasons of marital strife. Through the years of serving in the church, Joel and Mandy developed a strong passion for helping others build strong marriages which spawned this ministry, Marriage In Abundance.

Through many obstacles in life, God taught them—and is still teaching them—to use their marriage as an umbrella for protection from the storms in life. They desire the same for you!

Made in the USA
Monee, IL
15 February 2023